Gree...

NEW SURVEYS IN THE CLASSICS No. 42

HORACE

BY
S. J. HARRISON

Published for the Classical Association
CAMBRIDGE UNIVERSITY PRESS
2014

CAMBRIDGE UNIVERSITY PRESS
The Edinburgh Building, Cambridge CB2 8RU, United Kingdom
32 Avenue of the Americas, New York, NY 10013-2473, USA
477 Williamstown Road, Port Melbourne, VIC 3207, Australia
Ruiz de Alarcón 13, 28014 Madrid, Spain
Dock house, The Waterfront, Cape Town 8001, South Africa

www.cambridge.org
Information on this title: www.cambridge.org/9781107444447

Printed in the United Kingdom by Bell and Bain, Glasgow, UK

A catalogue record for this publication is available from the British Library

ISBN 9781107444447

.

CONTENTS

PREFACE

This volume sets out to replace the Horace New Survey by Gordon Williams of 1972, now more than forty years old. The preface to that book states that 'so much has been written about Horace even in the last decade that the mind wearies and sickens';[1] the last four decades have only increased the rate of production, and it is no longer possible to read even all the emerging scholarship on this most perennially popular of authors, let alone all the historic material. The splendid bibliography on Horace by Niklas Holzberg (2007, in print and online) contains over 2,500 items, mostly published since 1960; I have tried to map the broader tendencies in scholarship, largely listing books rather than articles, and I have concentrated on material published in the half-century since Eduard Fraenkel's *Horace* (1957). I have made liberal use of my own previous work on Horace.

The advent of the internet in the last generation has revolutionized classical scholarship, above all in bibliographical research, and in its first chapter this volume tries to direct the reader to the most relevant online resources. The same period has also seen a much increased interest in classical reception, which I have pursued for Horace in the last chapter. The shape of the book overall is largely chronological, both for convenience and also to reflect the interest of modern scholarship in the self-constructed careers of ancient poets (see Harrison 2010).

I am most grateful to John Taylor for his kind invitation to write this volume, for his considerable patience in waiting for it amid the many pressures of my other obligations, and for his editorial care. Warm thanks also go to Tony Woodman for some timely and helpful comments, to Joanna Snelling for kind assistance in sourcing the cover illustration, and to Hester Higton for her excellent copy-editing.

I would like to dedicate this book to the memory of two friends and colleagues, great Horatians both, who died within a week of each other in May 2013: Robin Nisbet and David West.

Stephen Harrison
Oxford, September 2013

---

[1] Williams 1972: 4.

I RESOURCES FOR THE STUDY OF HORACE

1. Horace in the digital age

The internet now provides many prime resources for the study of Horace which make life considerably easier for the student and scholar of the poet, such as reliable and searchable online Latin texts,[1] bibliographies,[2] and prose and verse translations of all kinds,[3] as well as access to a wide range of modern and classic Horatian scholarship via digital versions of older works, Google Books, and journal databases such as JSTOR and Project MUSE (for subscribing institutions),[4] not to mention increasing numbers of monographs available via subscription to publishers' own websites.[5] These resources are growing continually and repay regular monitoring. But most Horatian scholarship is still to be found in printed form: here I give a brief survey of the most useful books for effective orientation in the modern study of Horace.

2. Printed bibliographies

The massive Horatian bibliography for 1936–75 in Kissel 1981 and its supplement for the years 1976–91 in Kissel 1994 are both valuable, as is the survey of Horatian bibliography for the years 1957–87 by Doblhofer (1992); especially useful for recent work is the fully indexed sequel to Kissel 1994, covering the years 1992–2005, in Holzberg 2007 (also available online). Full bibliographical listings (especially of work in Italian) on almost every Horatian subject are to be found in the

---

[1] E.g. the PHI database, <http://latin.packhum.org>; see also <http://www.thelatinlibrary.com/>.

[2] For example, that by Niklas Holzberg (see section 2 below), currently (March 2014) available at <http://www.niklasholzberg.com/Homepage/Bibliographien.html>, and that by Wilfried Stroh, currently at <http://stroh.userweb.mwn.de/bibl/horaz.html>, or McNeill 2009 on *Oxford Bibliographies Online* at <http://www.oxfordbibliographies.com/>.

[3] E.g. various historical versions on the Perseus Digital Library, <http://www.perseus.tufts.edu/hopper>, or the modern version by A. S. Kline on his useful *Poetry in Translation* site, <http://www.poetryintranslation.com>.

[4] <http://www.jstor.org/> and <http://muse.jhu.edu/>.

[5] E.g. *Oxford Scholarship Online*, <http://www.oxfordscholarship.com/>, where many recent Oxford University Press books and some from other university presses can be found; also <http://www.cambridge.org/online/>, for Cambridge University Press.

Enciclopedia oraziana (Mariotti 1996–8; see section 4 below). The general online bibliography by McNeill (2009) is more selective as its format requires, but contains useful brief comment on the items listed. Substantial bibliographical listings are also to be found in the three *Companions* to Horace discussed in section 4 below (Harrison 2007a, Davis 2010a, and Günther 2013a).

3. Texts, commentaries, and English translations

Texts

For Horace, as for most other classical authors, the nineteenth century had seen much fundamental work on textual transmission. The text of Keller and Holder (1899, second edition 1925) still gives the most elaborate *apparatus criticus* and most extensive reports of manuscript readings. These were incorporated into the naturally much more selective apparatus of the Oxford Classical Text of E. C. Wickham (1900), with its second edition by H. W. Garrod (1912). F. Vollmer followed Keller and Holder in seeing three groups among the variety of Horatian manuscripts in his Teubner edition (second edition 1912); this was reduced to two by F. Klingner in his third edition (1959). However, because of contamination, such classification can be misleading,[6] and when Klingner posits a third group (Q) which he regards as a conflation of his two main classes (Ξ and Ψ), his procedure has proved vulnerable to criticism;[7] Courtney (2013a) has recently firmly argued that the antiquity of many shared corruptions indicates that there was in effect a single ancient source for our modern transmission of Horace's non-hexameter works.

Many modern editions have consequently preferred to treat manuscripts individually in the *apparatus criticus* even if formally recognizing groupings: see, for example, the Leipzig Teubner of Borzák (1984). Shackleton Bailey's Stuttgart Teubner (1985) presents the evidence clearly by splitting up Klingner's Ξ group into its components but retaining the symbol Ψ for the more homogeneous second group. It is difficult for an editor of Horace to decide when to emend;[8] vulgate

---

[6] See Brink 1971: 12–27.
[7] See Tarrant 1983.
[8] See Tränkle 1993.

readings are usually those of ancient editions and seldom incomprehensible, and Horace's style is often terse and testing. Many modern editors have been too conservative; Shackleton Bailey 1985 is sometimes too bold but is always stimulating.[9] A new Oxford Classical Text is planned by R. J. Tarrant, who will approach the manuscripts individually and eclectically, and who has suggested that what we need is a clearly comprehensible apparatus like that of Shackleton Bailey, but with fuller information on both manuscript readings and conjectures.[10]

Commentaries[11]

The ancient commentaries of pseudo-Acro and Porphyrio, though seldom as valuable as the ancient commentaries on Virgil, have been fully studied in recent years (on Acro see Noske 1969, on Porphyrio see Diederich 1999 and Kalinina 2007); in both cases a new text is a keen *desideratum* (for that of Acro see still Keller 1902, for Porphyrio Holder 1894). In terms of modern commentaries, the nineteenth century left a substantial legacy: particularly notable (and still of use) are the scholarly commentaries on the complete works by Wickham (1874, 1891), Kiessling (1884, 1886, 1889), and Keller and Holder (1899, especially rich in parallels), and the school commentary on the *Odes* by T. E. Page (1886). The twentieth century has built on these foundations, especially in Heinze's revision of Kiessling (last revised 1930, reprinted until 1960). Important too is the commentary on the *Satires* by Lejay (1911), still the fullest on that work.

In 1969 the short but stimulating commentary on the third book of the *Odes* by Gordon Williams appeared, and in the next year the massive commentary on Book 1 of the *Odes* by Nisbet and Hubbard (1970), with Book 2 following in 1978. This highly detailed editing of separate books broke new ground for the *Odes*: it reflected both an approach to ancient poems as individual literary artefacts open to judgement, and also the scholarly concern of Pasquali (1920) and Fraenkel (1957) with the Greek (and other) intertextualities of Horace's poetry in the *Odes*.

---

[9] See Nisbet 1986; Delz 1988. For a survey of editions up to Shackleton Bailey, see Tränkle 1993.

[10] I paraphrase a lecture by him at Cambridge, 10 January 2013.

[11] Commentaries are dealt with in more detail in the chapters dedicated to individual works below; these paragraphs are intended to give some rapid orientation.

The result was a need for a greater length of explanation than was permitted in the standard complete editions. Nisbet and Hubbard's concern with literary genre and category, and their lengthy collections of relevant parallels, following and extending the work of Keller and Holder, revealed how the literary tradition is moulded and reshaped in the *Odes* and set a scholarly standard for all subsequent commentaries on Latin poets, while their forthright literary views have provided stimulating points of departure for literary discussion.

The kind of detail which this depth of exegesis allows is further exemplified by Brink's vast edition of the *Ars poetica* and *Epistles* 2 (1963, 1971, 1982), which explores the language, meanings, and structure of these poems to a degree previously unparalleled in classical scholarship. Similarly scholarly and inclusive are the major commentary on the *Epodes* by Watson (2003), now required reading for detailed study of those poems, and the extensive commentary on *Odes* 4 by Fedeli and Ciccarelli (2008). The substantial running commentaries on the *Satires* and *Epistles* by Fedeli (1994, 1997) are of considerable interest for their literary analyses.

But the shorter commentary has not been neglected either, supplying the need for convenient school and university editions. In Italy there are many such editions: I would select for special mention Labate 1981 on the *Satires* and Cavarzere 1992 on the *Epodes*. In English, Quinn (1980) has produced a lively if uneven commentary on the *Odes* for students, with some interesting reactions to Nisbet and Hubbard; Rudd (1989) has capably summarized and varied Brink on *Epistles* 2 and the *Ars poetica*; and Brown (1993) and Muecke (1993) have produced Aris and Phillips editions of *Satires* 1 and 2 respectively, with parallel translations which are of considerable help in interpretation. Notably helpful are the three volumes of briefer commentary (with facing translation) by West on the first three books of the *Odes* (1995, 1998, 2002), which provide firm and lively interpretations of the key points in each poem. Several recent commentaries have appeared in the Cambridge 'Green and Yellow' series on Horatian books, following Rudd 1989: Mayer's commentary on *Epistles* 1 (1994) and Mankin's commentary on the *Epodes* (1995), the first editions of these poems in English for a generation;[12] Thomas' commentary on *Odes* 4 and the *Carmen saeculare* (2011); Gowers' commentary on *Satires* 1 (2012); and Mayer's on *Odes* 1

---

[12] Though some credit should be given to Dilke 1954, the commentary on *Epistles* 1 for generations of students.

(2012). Further commentaries are in progress in this series by myself on *Odes* 2 and by Freudenburg on *Satires* 2.

More interpretative running commentaries have also been produced; the most important of these is Syndikus 1972–3 (third edition 2001) on the *Odes* – succinct but pointed short essays on each poem which repeatedly identify the central points and problems and judiciously weigh up solutions. Particular strengths are a solid awareness of structure and of literary sources and allusions. Also significant in this genre is Putnam 1986 on *Odes* 4, where the stress is always on the artistically crafted verbal icon and on close reading of imagery and emotional colour, and a further running commentary on the same book by T. Johnson (2004), who argues that Book 4 effectively combines symposiastic and encomiastic elements, and who provides firm historical contextualization, a neat complement to Putnam's approach.

English translations

English translations of classical texts are a flourishing genre, and are increasingly executed as well as annotated or introduced by professional classicists: this is a positive tendency in applying scholarly expertise to public benefit, especially if (as in the case of Horace) the relevant scholars are also fluent writers in English. The major prose translations in print are that of Rudd of the *Odes* and *Epodes* in the Loeb series with parallel Latin text (Rudd 2004), and that of the *Satires* and *Epistles* by Davie in the World's Classics series (Davie 2011): both can be recommended as accurate, clear and elegant; those of *Satires* 1 and 2 by Brown and Muecke (see under 'Commentaries above') are also helpful. The standard verse translations are the World's Classics version of the *Odes* and *Epodes* by West (1997), and the Penguin Classics version of the *Satires* and *Epistles* by Rudd (revised version 1987), both accurate and well expressed. These are the key modern versions; others will be discussed in Chapter VII below, along with the historical tradition and the reception of Horace in general.

4. *Companions* and general accounts

Horace has been a particular beneficiary of the recent tendency in classical publishing to commission multi-contributor *Companions* to particular authors aimed at providing a synoptic view, with three such volumes now in print from Cambridge (Harrison 2007a), Wiley-Blackwell (Davis 2010a), and Brill (Günther 2013a). Between them these three volumes assemble most of the best-known Horatian scholars and provide a good range of different approaches. The Cambridge companion has shorter and briefer chapters, seeking to cover a wide range of topics and receptions as well as the usual analyses of particular poetic collections. The Wiley-Blackwell volume has less range but allows longer chapters and deeper excavation on certain topics, including substantial work on reception. The Brill volume, for its part, is the longest but pursues a more traditional path, containing detailed readings of Horace's works in a limited number of extensive literary chapters, plus sections on style and transmission. These volumes are the best starting point for anyone who wants to appreciate current directions in Horatian research.

Alongside these handbooks stands the *Enciclopedia oraziana* (Mariotti 1996–8), in three volumes each of about a thousand pages, which contain a plethora of entries in Italian on the poet on every topic from transmission to modern reception, occasionally of uneven quality but with detailed bibliography in almost every case. Its high price means that it can only be consulted in leading libraries, but it provides copious material and gives an excellent idea of the range of research on Horace in Italian (naturally better covered than other scholarly languages) up to the mid-1990s, and forms a suitable monument for the bimillennium of the poet's death in 1992/3.

General books by single authors covering the whole of Horace's output in the last half-century have necessarily laboured under the still considerable shadow of Fraenkel (1957), whose work has been formally marked as epoch-making by Doblhofer 1992. The book begins with the life of Horace and then goes through his works in chronological order, reflecting Fraenkel's general view that Horace's later work marks the heights of his development as a poet, especially in *Odes* 4, regarded by Fraenkel as a triumphant climax. The great strength of the book lies in its close analysis of individual poems, bringing out their sources, structures, and other important elements; perhaps the most outstanding of these is the famous treatment of *Odes* 3.4 as an imitation of Pindar's first *Pythian* ode. Such detailed treatment necessitates selection, but Fraenkel manages to deal with a high proportion of Horace's poems. His omissions are instructive: on the one hand most of the lighter erotic odes, on the other the *Ars poetica* and *Epistles* 2.2. The former are left out since they do not fit

Fraenkel's picture of the dignified and serious poet, the latter because their fluid dating does not allow a neat placing in the development of Horace's career which forms the frame of the book. A central theme of the book is Horace's relationship with Augustus, one of developing admiration and respect according to Fraenkel, who sees *Odes* 4.5 (his favourite Horatian poem) as the final and most exquisite expression of the poet's loyal affection. Though much is dated in the overall approach, the unity of Fraenkel's vision and the quality of his scholarly analysis remain impressive half a century later.

Fraenkel's book seems to have deterred others from large-scale general treatments; since 1957 there have been mainly short books of this kind, such as Grimal 1958 and Perret 1959 (English translation 1964), both of which give capable summaries of Horace's career with some interesting literary judgements, West 1967, La Penna 1969, and Williams 1972. La Penna directly opposes Fraenkel, arguing that the 'real' Horace is the ethical private poet rather than the public bard; West explores in some depth the imagery and thought-sequence of select passages of Horace, offering a model of practical criticism which is sometimes over-ingenious but always intelligent and thought-provoking. Williams, in the forerunner to this volume and following the format of this series, provides a survey of issues and problems in Horace which usefully reacts against a number of Fraenkel's more arguable views.

The biographical model has remained attractive to some after Fraenkel, especially in books intended for a broader audience. Levi 1997 looks back specifically to Fraenkel in its structure, close readings, and presentation of Horace as historical personality (and has some good translations by the author, a noted poet). Hills 2005 and Holzberg 2009 both move through the works of Horace chronologically, but concentrate more on reading the poems as works of literature rather than as expressions of personality and traces of biography: Hills is a lively short treatment for the general reader, but written by a scholar well up with recent developments, while Holzberg shows a particular interest in the unity and development of Horace's work and the structuring of his individual poetry collections. Armstrong 1989 again goes through the works in order, with many lively interpretative comments for the general reader, and some important arguments about Horace's social background, conveniently reprised in Armstrong 2010. Sophisticated and nuanced modifications of the biographical tendency can be found in Lyne 1995, who argues that Horace's public poetry throughout his career combines the required encomium of the great with more personal and subversive views, and in Oliensis 1998, who sees Horace's work as concerned primarily with rhetorical self-presentation and 'saving face' amid the pressures of Roman society and the desire for literary fame.

A number of significant volumes collect studies on Horace by single hands. Shackleton Bailey 1982 is a mixed collection of essays, with a stress on interpretative difficulties, appropriate to an editor of Horace; while Büchner's collection of interpretations (1962) contains a number of papers which are strong on technical and linguistic analysis. The collected Horatian papers of Klingner (1953, 1964) treat both transmission and literary interpretation, and show a depth and sympathy of interpretation which influenced both Nisbet and Hubbard and Syndikus. La Penna 1993 gathers an important and influential body of work which presents Horace as an artist struggling to maintain personal independence under political pressure to praise Augustus. Equally significant is the body of work in Schmidt 2002b, with its interest in pronouncedly ethical and highly aesthetic readings of the poems with some good close analysis, in formal structures in Horace's poems and poetry books, and in the considerable reception of Horace in German literature.[13] Woodman 2012 contains a number of literary essays on Horace, especially on his interaction with historiography, while Cairns 2012 collects many articles on the *Odes*.

Further volumes collect studies by different scholars, another recent tendency, often reflecting the proceedings of a conference. An early case (in a significant series) was Costa 1973, containing stimulating pieces by Hubbard and West on the *Odes* and Russell on the *Ars poetica*. The bimillennium of Horace's birth in 1992/3 yielded (apart from the *Enciclopedia oraziana*) some significant collections: Rudd 1993a, Ludwig 1993a, Harrison 1995a (covering a range of Horatian topics), and Martindale and Hopkins 1993 (a key gathering of essays on the reception of Horace – see further in Chapter VII). More recently, Woodman and Feeney 2002 gathers together new pieces by major Horatian scholars across the range of Horace's work, and the two volumes of reprinted papers on Horace in the Oxford Readings in Classical Studies series have brought together some classic pieces with excellent contextualizing introductions (Freudenburg 2009, Lowrie 2009a); other useful similar collections are Santirocco 1994 and Anderson 1999.

---

[13] For a detailed account see Harrison 2002.

II LIFE, POETIC CAREER, SELF-PRESENTATION

1. Life

A brief life of Horace survives from the ancient world, attached to the name of Suetonius and probably summarizing a longer life by that writer,[1] which is worth quoting in full here.[2]

Quintus Horatius Flaccus of Venusia had for a father, as he himself writes, a freedman who was a collector of money at auctions; but it is believed that he was a dealer in salted provisions, for a certain man in a quarrel thus taunted Horace: 'How often have I seen your father wiping his nose with his arm!' Horace served as military tribune in the war of Philippi, at the instance of Marcus Brutus, one of the leaders in that war. When his party was vanquished, he was pardoned and purchased the position of quaestor's clerk (*scriptus quaestorius*). Then contriving to win the favour, first of Maecenas and later of Augustus, he held a prominent place among the friends of both. How fond Maecenas was of him is evident enough from the well-known epigram: 'If I did not love you, my own Horace, more than my own vitals, you would see your dear friend leaner than Ninnius.' But he expressed himself much more strongly in his last will and testament in this brief remark to Augustus: 'Be as mindful of Horatius Flaccus as of myself.'

Augustus offered him the post of secretary, as appears in this letter of his to Maecenas: 'Before this I was able to write my letters to my friends with my own hand; now overwhelmed with work and in poor health, I desire to take our friend Horace from you. He will come then from that parasitic table of yours to my kingly one, and help me write my letters.' Even when Horace declined, Augustus showed no resentment at all, and did not cease his efforts to gain his friendship. We have letters from which I append a few extracts by way of proof: 'Enjoy any privilege at my house, as if you were making your home there; for it will be quite right and proper for you to do so, inasmuch as that was the relation which I wished to have with you, if your health had permitted.' And again, 'How mindful I am of you our friend Septimius can also tell you; for it chanced that I spoke of you in his presence. Even if you were so proud as to scorn my friendship, I do not therefore return your disdain.' Besides this, among other pleasantries, he often called him 'the cleanest of willies' and 'his charming little man', and he made him well to do by more than one act of generosity.

As to his writings, Augustus rated them so high, and was so convinced that they would be immortal, that he not only appointed him to write the *Carmen saeculare*, but also asked him to celebrate the victory of his stepsons Tiberius and Drusus over the Vindelici, and so compelled him to add a fourth to his three books of *Odes* after a

---

[1] For its origin, see still Fraenkel 1957: 1–13. Text and translation are most easily found in Rolfe 1914: 484–91.

[2] Translation from Fairclough 1927, modified.

long silence. Furthermore, after reading several of his *sermones*, the Emperor thus complained that no mention was made of him: 'You must know that I am not pleased with you, that in your numerous writings of this kind you do not talk with me, rather than with others. Are you afraid that your reputation with posterity will suffer because it appears that you were my friend?' In this way he forced from Horace the selection which begins with these words: 'Seeing that single-handed you bear the burden of tasks so many and so great, protecting Italy's realm with arms, providing it with morals, reforming it by laws, I should sin against the public good, Caesar, if I wasted your time with long discourse [*Epist.* 2.1].'

In person he was short and fat, as he is described by himself in his *Satires* and by Augustus in the following letter: 'Onysius has brought me your little volume, and I accept it, small as it is, in good part, as an apology. But you seem to me to be afraid that your books may be bigger than you are yourself; but it is only stature that you lack, not girth. So you may write on a pint pot, that the circumference of your volume may be well rounded out, like that of your own belly.'

It is said that he was unrestrained in matters of sex; for it is reported that in a room lined with mirrors he had prostitutes so arranged that whichever way he looked, he saw a reflection of the sexual act. He lived for the most part in the country in the retirement of his Sabine or Tiburtine estate, and his house is pointed out near the little grove of Tiburnus. There came into my hands some elegies ascribed to him and a letter in prose, supposed to be a recommendation of himself to Maecenas, but I think that both are spurious; for the elegies are commonplace and the letter is even obscure, which was by no means one of his faults.

He was born on the sixth day before the Ides of December in the consulate of Lucius Cotta and Lucius Torquatus, and died on the fifth day before the Kalends of the same month in the consulship of Gaius Marcius Censorinus and Gaius Asinius Gallus, fifty-nine days after the death of Maecenas, in his fifty-seventh year. He named Augustus as his heir in his physical presence, since he could not make and sign a will because of the sudden violence of his illness. He was buried and laid to rest near the tomb of Maecenas on the furthest part of the Esquiline hill.

This is the key source for the basic data about Horace: his birthday (8 December 65 BCE; for confirmation of the month see *Epist.* 1.10.27), his birthplace (Venusia, modern Venosa, on the border of ancient Apulia and Lucania – *Sat.* 2.1.34–5), and his date of death (27 November 8 BCE). Most of its information is taken either from Horace's own works or from the (now lost) works of others such as Augustus and Maecenas. His father's career as auctioneer and financial agent and his freedman status is confirmed by *Satires* 1.6:[3] it seems likely that he was freed after temporary enslavement as a captive in the Social War,[4] and in later life the father seems to have made enough

---

[3] The unlikely idea that Horace's father was Jewish and from Alexandria has recently been revived for discussion by Newman 2011: 446–58.

[4] See Williams 1995.

money to send his son to the prestigious school of Orbilius at Rome (*Sat.* 1.6.76–8, *Epist.* 2.1.71) and later to Athens for university-style study with the sons of the Roman elite (*Epist.* 2.2.43–5).

It was there that he attached himself to the cause of Brutus, who was in Athens studying philosophy in the months after the Ides of March (Plutarch, *Brutus* 24.1), and went with him on campaign in Greece, and perhaps in Asia too (*Sat.* 1.7?), serving as *tribunus militum* (*Sat.* 1.6.48), a rank for the young elite. In the autumn of 42 BCE he was on the losing side in the crushing defeat of Brutus at Philippi at the hands of Antony and the young Caesar (*Odes* 2.7), but escaped and returned to Rome, where he was able to buy the post of *scriba quaestorius*, a significant administrative position which he seems to have retained at least to the end of the 30s BCE (*Sat.* 2.6.36–7). In the early 30s he became attached to the circle of writers around Augustus' important adviser Maecenas, introduced by no less than Virgil (*Sat.* 2.6.40–2, 1.6.55–6), and for the next thirty years this was his key social group; it is now clear that several of these poets, including Horace, were linked with the Epicurean philosopher and poet Philodemus.[5]

Recent writing on the life of Horace has stressed that the poet's own presentation of his financial position after Philippi exaggerates his losses: though he claims that he lost his father's land, perhaps in the land confiscations of 41–40 BCE, and turned to poetry to make money (*Epist.* 2.2.49–52), he seems to have been able to buy his post as quaestor's clerk without special trouble, and any financial embarrassment must have been over by the 30s, when he was clearly of equestrian status and substantially wealthy.[6] Most modern scholars are clear, too, that Horace's financial position after the 30s was bolstered by the gift of a substantial Sabine estate from Maecenas, which contained several subordinate farms as well as a villa (*Sat.* 2.6), the remains of which are probably under the later grander building close to Licenza near Tivoli, which has been much investigated in recent years.[7] It is true that the poet never says in cold terms that the villa was Maecenas' gift (see further in section 3C below), but he expresses warm gratitude

---

[5] See Janko 2000:6.

[6] See e.g. Mayer 1995; Armstrong 2010.

[7] For the project of excavation see the details at <http://www.humnet.ucla.edu/horaces-villa/Contents.html>. For a brief printed summary see Frischer 2010, and for the full publication Frischer et al. 2006.

for the latter's generosity in enabling him to pursue a country existence (*Epist.* 1.7), and his poems tend to conceal the financial facts diplomatically while simultaneously acknowledging the consequent obligation in a form of gift economy.[8]

Horace's personal relations with Augustus seem to have been close, and perhaps became closer after 19 BCE when Augustus, who had been absent for much of the 20s, was generally in Rome: there seems no real reason to doubt the apparent documentary evidence of their intimacy in the Suetonian *Life*, especially since Suetonius would have had special access to the imperial archives given his administrative posts under Trajan and Hadrian.[9] The presence of the *princeps* in Rome as active patron perhaps explains why Maecenas receives only one (warm) mention in Book 4 of the *Odes* against two poems addressed to Augustus and several celebrating members of his family, and no mention at all in Horace's latest works, *Epistles* 2 and the *Ars poetica* (see below). The idea that Maecenas fell from grace in connection with a plot against Augustus at the end of the 20s is now believed by few, and it is not clear whether he 'retired' in any sense as a patron of poets.[10] It may have been directly rather than through Maecenas that Horace was commissioned to write the *Carmen saeculare* for the *ludi saeculares* of 17 BCE, but this is unclear. There is no reason to disbelieve the Suetonian *Life* that Horace died less than two months after Maecenas in 8 BCE, temptingly close though this would be to assertions in the poetry that the poet would not wish to outlive his patron.

The main chronology and sequence of Horace's works is generally agreed. *Satires* 1 belongs to around 36/35 BCE,[11] *Satires* 2 and *Epodes* to around 30/29 BCE,[12] *Odes* 1–3 to 23 BCE,[13] *Epistles* 1 to 20/19 BCE,[14] the *Carmen saeculare* to 17 BCE, and *Odes* 4 to 14/13 BCE.[15] Two points have been recently debated: whether the three books of *Odes* 1–3 were each published separately prior to their collective publication in 23, and

[8] Bowditch 2001, 2010.

[9] See Wallace-Hadrill 1985: 73–96; Malcovati 1977.

[10] See Williams 1990; White 1991.

[11] See *Sat.* 1.10.86 with Gowers 2012: 336 (the presence of Bibulus in Rome in the winter of 36–35 is a dating point). In general, *Satires* 1 seems to belong to the period of peace after Naulochus (September 36).

[12] Both clearly after the deaths of Antony and Cleopatra in autumn 30 but before the triumphal return of the young Caesar in autumn 29.

[13] Though the usual marker of the suffect consulship of Sestius in 23 (Nisbet and Hubbard 1970: xxxv–vii) has now been doubted by Hutchinson 2008: 138.

[14] After Tiberius' Eastern settlement of 20 (*Epist.* 1.12.26–7): see Mayer 1994: 8–11.

[15] Before Augustus' return to Rome in 13: see *Odes* 4.5 and Thomas 2011: 5–7.

the continuing question of the dating of the second book of *Epistles* and the *Ars poetica*. A good case has been made for each of the books of *Odes* having a particular chronological range, with 1.4 perhaps predating Sestius' consulship of 23 and belonging to a book with no detectable dates after 26, Book 2 belonging to 25–24, and Book 3 to 23.[16] *Epistles* 2.1 is clearly dated to around 12 BCE, with its address of Augustus as sole ruler (after the death of Agrippa), but *Epistles* 2.2 has often been dated together with the first book of *Epistles*. This would create a two-poem book where the individual items may vary up to a decade in date, which seems strange.

Dates for the *Ars poetica* have varied considerably, but most scholars would now want to place it at the end of Horace's career as a final poetic statement. I have recently argued in detail (following a brief suggestion of Kilpatrick)[17] that *Epistles* 2.1 and 2.2 both belong to the period after 12 BCE and that they may have been combined with the *Ars poetica* in a single final book.[18] This thesis (the arguments for which are summarized in section 2D below) has found some acceptance and is at least an economic solution to the problem.

2. Poetic career

The tracing of the trajectory of Horace's poetic career has now to some degree displaced the reconstruction of his biography in contemporary scholarship. This seems justified, as most of the poet's traditional biography is hopefully reconstructed from the texts of the poems, which are complex literary artefacts rather than records of real life. Classical scholars share this interest in poetic careers with scholars of Renaissance literature, whose authors were of course responding to the evident self-fashioning of poetic careers by Virgil, Horace, and Ovid.[19] Interest in the phases of Horace's career has been an established theme since Becker, whose substantial book (Becker 1963) on the last period of Horace's literary production (after 23 BCE) argued for its unity as the work of a poet concerned with ethical principles. More recently

---

[16] See Hutchinson 2008: 131–61.
[17] Kilpatrick 1990: xi. Williams 1972: 38–9 also argued briefly that the three poems belonged in one book, but dated that book to soon after 17 BCE.
[18] Harrison 2008.
[19] See especially Hardie and Moore 2010.

Cucchiarelli 2001 has presented the early Horace of the *Satires* and *Epodes* as a poet of bodily concerns and comic tendencies, but also as sufficiently interested in generic variety to cross the bridge to the next section of his career in the lyric *Odes*. In the following section I give a personal account of Horace's poetic career which incorporates recent scholarship.[20]

A. Satires *1,* Satires *2, and* Epodes: *from outsider to insider*

The three earliest books of Horatian poetry begin from self-consciously low literary predecessors: *Satires* 1 and 2 pick up the hexameter *sermo* of Lucilius, the humble and parodic cousin of hexameter epic, looking at least momentarily to Attic Old Comedy as a Greek parallel (*Sat.* 1.4.1–6), while the *Epodes* take on the rumbustious and low-life world of archaic Archilochean iambus. This constructs a poetic career as beginning near the bottom of the generic scale: such self-positioning, along with the elements of aggression fundamental to both these low genres, nicely fits a poet who starts the period as an angry young man who has suffered real worldly dispossession. It has been well argued that within *Satires* 1 we find a kind of autobiographical progress of Horace from the excluded moralist of *Satires* 1.1–3 to the Maecenatic poet of 1.4 and beyond who has entered the literary establishment:[21] we move from the apparently isolated street preacher to the *amicus* of Maecenas in 1.5, 1.6, and 1.9, who in 1.10 takes his place among the leading writers of the day.

This trajectory comes out especially in the two literary catalogues of this concluding satire of Horace's first book. In the first of these, Horace looks to take his place among the master poets of his time just as he has taken his place among the *amici* of Maecenas (1.10.40–8, listing Fundanius for comedy, Pollio for tragedy, and Virgil for pastoral). Indeed, the social and the poetic circles are to some degree coextensive: in 1.6 Varius and Virgil are said to have introduced Horace to Maecenas, and all three are found in Maecenas' train in 1.5, while it is Fundanius who reports to Horace in *Satires* 2.8 the gastronomic excesses of the *cena Nasidieni* at which Fundanius himself, Varius, and Maecenas were all present. The implication of this passage

---

[20] This section incorporates parts of Harrison 2010.
[21] See Zetzel 1980; Gowers 2003.

is that Horace clearly places himself as the contemporary master of satire among the contemporary masters of other genres. The second catalogue is that of the critics whom Horace would like to please now that his poetic career is seriously under way (1.10.81–92, listing Plotius, Varius, Maecenas, Virgil, Valgius, Octavius, Fuscus, the Viscus brothers, Pollio, Messalla and his brother, Bibulus, Servius, and Furnius).

These lists obviously overlap, with Varius, Virgil, and Pollio appearing from the first one, but the second one addresses them in their critical rather than poetic capacity (like the poets of Hellenistic Alexandria, they are deemed to excel in both). Those added are partly further poet/ critics (Plotius Tucca, supposed co-editor of the *Aeneid*, and the elegist Valgius, later addressed in *Odes* 2.9), but also important contemporary patrons – Maecenas (of course), Messalla and his brother – as well as those known only as critics (Octavius, Fuscus, the brothers Visci, Bibulus, Servius, and Furnius). This catalogue of potential reviewers is the last item in *Satires* 1: Horace's first poetic book is offered for the approval (presumably forthcoming) of his literary colleagues.

This epilogue to critics may have been fashionable in the period: in what seems to be the final sequence of a book from his *Amores*, to be dated either to the mid-40s BCE or not long after Naulochus in 36,[22] the elegist Cornelius Gallus (interestingly not mentioned by Horace at all) likewise addresses Viscus and Cato, two of the critics named in *Satires* 1.10. A final appeal to critics seems then to be a standard gesture in Latin poetry of the triumviral period, and a standard way of marking the entrance of a new work, and in Horace's case of a new poet, whose literary career is now launched under impressive auspices.

In *Satires* 2 and the *Epodes* we find the first example of Horace's working on more than one poetic genre simultaneously. This 'horizontal' aspect is an interesting part of his poetic career: such an implicit self-construction as a poet who operates on more than one generic front suggests the *poikilia* or generic versatility for which Callimachus represents himself criticized in the first of his *Iambi*, a collection which is certainly significant for Horace's *Epodes*.[23] *Satires* 2 itself shows only a little overt contact with the *Epodes*: its mention of Canidia in its final line (2.8.95) is presumably a clever allusion to the ending of the simultaneous *Epodes*, in the last poem of which (17) Canidia makes her most extensive appearance.

[22] fr.2 Courtney, *FLP*, lines 6–9; for the classic discussion see Anderson et al. 1979.
[23] See Watson 2003: 12–17.

In general, the second book of the *Satires* reinforces the 'vertical' aspect of Horace's poetic career: five years or so on from *Satires* 1, he can open his new *sermo*-collection by implying that not just Maecenas but also Caesar is a supporter. *Satires* 1.1 began with an address to Maecenas, but *Satires* 2.1, addressed to the lawyer Trebatius, has as its first major topic a discussion of whether Horace should address Caesar directly (10–20) and ends with the poet's self-characterization as *laudatus Caesare*, 'praised by Caesar' (84). Maecenas himself has to wait for mention until the end of 2.3 (2.3.312), though he re-emerges in the last three poems of the book, especially in 2.6, effectively a thank-offering for the gift of the Sabine estate (see also 2.7.33 and the dinner-party of 2.8, mentioned above). The implicit support of Caesar through the *amicitia* of Maecenas in Book 1 is replaced by direct praise of the great man.

This apparent social elevation after the ascent of Book 1 is matched by a literary elevation. *Satires* 2 has only eight poems to the ten of *Satires* 1: this is mainly because of *Satires* 2.3 (a vast 326 lines), where the Stoic Damasippus comically fails to stick to Stoic brevity in his philosophical exposition. Such impressive length (even if parodic here) was not found in *Satires* 1, not least because that book criticized Lucilius for his prolixity and promoted Callimachean polish and brevity, and it represents a Horace unafraid to expand, even parodically. *Satires* 2 also contains a wholesale epic parody in 2.5, a rewriting of Odysseus' underworld consultation with Tiresias in *Odyssey* 11 as a set of instructions on how to repair an impaired fortune by *captatio* or legacy-hunting. This return to a traditional feature of Lucilius naturally stresses the affinity of satire with the higher genre of epic as its lower twin, only implicitly stated in *Satires* 1.

As already noted, this ascent between the two books of *Satires* is accompanied by the simultaneous emergence of Horace as an iambic poet in the *Epodes*. In generic terms this is again an ascent: the lowly *musa pedestris*, 'muse that travels on foot', of satire (*Satires* 2.6.17) and the self-image of Horatian *sermo* as not really lofty enough to be poetry (see section 3 below) mean that even the bluff, aggressive, and sometimes pornographic persona of Archilochus is a move up because of his undoubted status as a vigorous and inspired poet. As scholars have noted, Horace's version of Archilochus is toned down and less 'potent' than the original,[24] but once again we find the Horatian literary career paralleling his socio-political positioning. Though published

---

[24] See Watson 1995.

after Actium, the *Epodes* show the whole extent of the movement from outsider to insider: the aggressive, Archilochean analyses of the ills of Rome in *Epodes* 7 and 16, which have plausibly been suggested as the poems which triggered Horace's recruitment into the Maecenatic circle,[25] turn into equally Archilochean celebrations of the victory at Actium in *Epodes* 1 and 9, both addressed in warm terms to Maecenas, which recall Archilochus' poems of friendship and ship-board action in war.[26]

This 'vertical' aspect of the *Epode* book is matched with the evident turn in its second part towards an interest in higher literary genres. As scholars have shown, the *Epodes'* opening sequence of ten poems in a strongly Archilochean metre is followed by a group of poems which look to other genres (11–14).[27] *Epode* 11, with its presentation of the *exclusus amator* ('locked-out lover'), and *Epode* 14, with its helpless lover, both evoke typical figures of Roman elegy, perhaps drawn from the lost *Amores* of Gallus, famously alluded to in the last poem (*Ecl.* 10) of Virgil's *Eclogues*, published in 38 BCE. On the other hand, *Epode* 13, with its scenario of a landscape description with a storm motivating a sympotic occasion and moralizing reflections, famously represents a striking anticipation of *Odes* 1.9 (the Soracte poem). Just as Virgil had been instrumental in Horace's social career in introducing him to Maecenas (*Satires* 1.6.54–5), so the same poet's first published poetry book (briefly commended as we have seen at *Satires* 1.10.44–5) exercises considerable influence over this first phase of Horace's poetic career. The ten poems of *Satires* 1 may follow the number of poems in the *Eclogues*,[28] while *Epode* 2 and *Epode* 16 plainly interact with the collection's poetic world: the praise of the rural life ironized in the former has clear elements drawn from Virgilian bucolic, while the fantastic dimension of the Islands of the Blest in the latter inverts in pessimistic mode the optimistic pastoral fantasies of the prophecy of *Eclogue* 4.[29]

This first and formative phase of Horace's poetic career, then, is marked by a rhetoric of literary and socio-political ascent. Horace rises from the humble exponent of rough Lucilian satire, refining it in Callimachean terms, through Archilochean iambus, tempered for

[25] See Nisbet 1984.
[26] See Harrison 2007b: 106–14.
[27] See Harrison 2007b: 119–30.
[28] See Zetzel 1980.
[29] See Harrison 2007b: 130–4.

new times, to the brink of lyric operations, matching his movement from Republican defeat at Philippi and loss of property to the generous patronage of Maecenas and political engagement with the interests of the young Caesar. This vertical element is counterbalanced by a horizontal axis: Horace's simultaneous collections in *Satires* 2 and the *Epodes* look out not only to each other but also to the contemporary poetic scene sketched in detail at the end of *Satires* 1.10. Horace has arrived among the poets of triumviral Rome, and is concerned to negotiate his space on the current literary horizon by interacting with its important strands. As we shall discover, all these elements will continue in the lyric project of *Odes* 1–3.

B. Odes *1–3 and* Epistles *1: the turn to lyric and the first return to* sermo

Though it is possible, as we have seen, that it was also published serially in single books,[30] the collection of *Odes* 1–3 which emerged as a unit about 23 BCE must be conceived as a single stage in Horace's poetic career. Its opening and closing poems, *Odes* 1.1 and 3.30, share a metre (stichic first Asclepiad) not otherwise used in the eighty-eight odes of the three books, and the latter poem is clearly a pendant to the former. At the end of 1.1, itself constructed on the basis of a priamel framework from early Greek lyric, Horace famously asks for inclusion in the canon of Greek lyric poets (1.1.29–36), and at the end of 3.30 he suggests that he has done enough to deserve this (3.30.10–16).

One subject of justifiable pride in Horace's lyric achievement in *Odes* 1–3 is the dexterous employment of choriamb-based Greek lyric metres, harder to accomplish in Latin with its greater number of long syllables, something made even harder by Horatian tightening of the archaic rules.[31] This is clearly an ascent in complexity from the simple hexameters of the two books of *Satires* and the identical epodic metres of *Epodes* 1–10, though the more mixed metres of *Epodes* 11–17 (one of which – the first Archilochean – reappears in the *Odes*: *Epode* 12 = *Odes* 1.7 and 1.28) are some kind of anticipation of this move. This metrical prowess is famously stressed by the use of nine different metres for the first nine odes, followed by a sequence of poems (12–18) in which thematic elements appear from an identifiable range of individual Greek

---

[30] See Hutchinson 2008: 131–61.
[31] See Nisbet and Hubbard 1970: xxxviii–xlvi.

lyric poets.[32] This appreciable technical step in Horace's career is thus strongly marked in a major group of initial poems.

Between the challenge of *Odes* 1.1 and its fulfilment in *Odes* 3.30, there is some sense of internal ascent and onward movement. While I do not fully subscribe to general interpretations of *Odes* 1–3 which regard their order as completely plotted by their author with narrative significance,[33] some element of progress through the collection seems clear. The initial window-display of the adaptation of Greek lyric through metre and themes just noted is followed in Book 2 by a more moderate approach to both metre and subject matter:[34] a set of topics in which moral philosophy is prominent is treated in twenty poems which in the first ten simply alternate the commonest Horatian lyric metres (the Alcaic and Sapphic stanzas). As the book comes to a close, it shows some anticipation of the national and grave themes of the Roman Odes at the beginning of Book 3: in particular, 2.18, with its criticism of luxury and commendation of the poet's own modest sufficiency in the Sabine estate, looks forward to themes from *Odes* 3.1.

In *Odes* 3, there is a clear elevation of content:[35] the opening sequence of six lengthy Roman Odes tackles major themes of politics and public morality in an enigmatic style which combines a vatic, oracular stance with elements of higher poetic genres. *Odes* 3.3 gives a version of the divine assembly approving the apotheosis of Romulus from Ennius' *Annales*, while *Odes* 3.5 tells the story of Regulus, likely to have been treated in the account of the first Punic War in Naevius' *Bellum Punicum*. Several other poems later in the book narrate myths associated with tragedy (Hypermestra in 3.11, Danae in 3.16) or epyllion (Europa in 3.27), and the lofty tone and impressive length of 3.24 and its address to a generalized reader pick up the initial Roman Odes symmetrically towards the book's end, just as 3.29 combines Roman Ode-style length and moralizing with a final address to Maecenas before the epilogue of 3.30. Here, in the final book of the first collection of *Odes*, Horatian lyric reaches its most elevated literary texture: though the *Carmen saeculare* and *Odes* 4 address equally lofty subject matter, in Horace's subsequent poetic career his mid-life lyric achievement seems to represent his finest moment, and his lasting

---

[32] See Lowrie 1995.

[33] See D. Porter 1987 for an extreme version of this thesis, Santirocco 1986 for a milder one.

[34] See Harrison 2010.

[35] See Lowrie 1997: 224–316.

reputation is presented as that of the Roman Alcaeus (*Epist.* 2.2.99), a clear allusion to his extensive use of that poet in Books 1–3 of the *Odes* (see most explicitly 1.32) rather than to Book 4, where Alcaeus is barely present.

The first book of *Epistles* presents a conscious contrast with the first collection of *Odes*, which it follows a few years later. Its opening programmatic poem claims that Horace has renounced the frivolities of poetry for the serious concerns of philosophy (1.1.7–12). The pose of not writing poetry is surely ironic in this book of carefully crafted hexameters, and forms part of a consistent ambiguity about the poetic status of Horatian *sermo* (is it 'really' poetry? See further in Section 3 below). The collection's overt shape as a letter collection, though picking up epistolary elements in Lucilius, points to a genre of prose literature, as does its philosophical content (though one should not underestimate the influence of Lucretius' philosophical poem). In terms of Horace's poetic career, however, *Epistles* 1 represents a conscious return to the *sermo* of the 30s, in a slicker, more varied poetry book: the greater number of items (20 in *Epistles* 1 as opposed to 10 and 8 in *Satires* 1 and 2) reflects not only the relative brevity conventional for the letter but also a poet who has in the last decade produced eighty-eight lyric poems in three books.

The turn from Horatian lyric form is matched by a partial turn from Horatian lyric *persona*. Though Horace can still describe himself as *Epicuri de grege porcum* ('a porker from Epicurus' herd', *Epist.* 1.4.16) and can still suggest (in the same poem, at 1.4.13) that each day should be treated as one's last in the true Epicurean style, the poet's hedonistic involvement in the sympotic and erotic world of *Odes* 1–3 has indeed vanished, and he is presented as a trainee moral philosopher who encourages his friends along the same road by appearing equally fallible rather than a stern and superior sage.

The themes of love, drinking, and politics linked with lyric in the style of Alcaeus (*Odes* 1.32.1–12) are replaced by concerns with ethics, friendship, and patronage, all part of moral philosophy in Roman terms. This is best seen in two pairs of poems where an addressee is shared between the two collections. Horace's friend Fuscus can be teased for his Stoicism in both *Odes* 1.22 and *Epistles* 1.10, but where the former poem then turns to Horace's own comic love affair with Lalage, the latter develops an ethical argument about living according to nature. Likewise, the Quinctius invited to put away political concerns and attend a symposium in *Odes* 2.11 is in *Epistles* 1.16 called (via a description of Horace's Sabine estate) to match good reputation with good actions and determined moral character. Similarly, the political themes prominent in *Odes* 1–3 and soon to be central to *Odes* 4 are introduced only briefly and incidentally: the military doings of Agrippa, Tiberius, and Augustus are added as mere epistolary topical references at the end of *Epistle* 1.12 (25–9), while Augustus is further alluded to only in celebrating his birthday (*Epist.* 1.5) and as a present-ee of the first collection of Odes (*Epist.* 1.13).

The last two poems of the first book of *Epistles* stress further this more relaxed and less grand self-presentation of the philosophical and self-ironizing poet. In 1.19, Horace, in a poem which wittily uses the idea of the drunken poet to pick up the sympotic themes of the *Odes*, asserts his literary importance as the introducer of Archilochean iambus and Lesbian lyric in Latin, taking stock of his poetic career so far while ignoring *sermo* as less important (1.19.21–34). But as so often (see section 3 below), this proud claim is counterbalanced by Horatian self-irony: the poem closes with the comic picture of Horace's determined avoidance of poetic recitation (1.19.35–49), and the collection's final piece takes up the witty conceit of addressing its own poetry book as if it were a slave-boy destined to lose its bloom and beauty through sexual experience. Both poem and book end with an ambivalent autobiography which provides the personal counterpart to the poetic career sketched in 1.19 (1.20.19–28), presenting for the reader's approval Horace's struggle from an unpromising back-ground and early setbacks to the position of friend of Maecenas and Augustus. The marking here of his forty-fourth birthday in December 21 BCE is not so much a date for the book (which must have appeared in 20/19) as a parallel to the normal public career of the elite Roman: Horace has passed the usual consular age (forty-two in the Late Republic), and here sets himself as a private citizen with per-sonal foibles and achievements against the consuls who would normally be his coevals. Just as *Epistles* 1.1 represented Horace as renouncing poetry, so the final poem in the same book presents him as a private individual in the context of the public magistracies of the Roman state.

C. Carmen saeculare *and* Odes *4: return to lyric*

Horace's commission to write a lyric poem (conventionally labelled the *Carmen saeculare*) for performance by a mixed choir of boys and girls at

Augustus' ideologically crucial *ludi saeculares* of 17 BCE, celebrating the renewal of the *saeculum* or generation of 110 years, represents an anomaly in his career: it is a one-off lyric piece outside a collection, and it is written in a choral rather than a monodic mode.[36] Its link with the Greek lyric genre of paean is clear, but its importance in Horace's poetic career is not so much for its literary qualities as for its status as an occasional poem commissioned for an express politico-religious occasion; the ancient life of Horace attributed to Suetonius suggests the hand of the *princeps* himself in Horace's selection. The death of Virgil in 19 BCE had left Horace as the unchallenged chief poet of Rome, and the *Carmen saeculare* clearly presents him as a kind of laureate, addressing the gods on behalf of the Roman state on a public occasion of the highest profile.

This externally motivated resumption of Horatian lyric clearly led to a further period of production in the genre (this time in its monodic form), which culminated in the fourth book of fifteen odes a few years later. Whether or not (as the Suetonian *Life* suggests – see section 1 above) Augustus himself stimulated this sequel collection by requesting the poems in praise of the victories of his stepsons Tiberius and Drusus (*Odes* 4.4 and 4.14), the character of this last lyric book is distinctly different from that of the first three. Book 4 begins by figuring itself as a return to love (and therefore lyric love poetry), presented as inappropriate for a man past fifty (4.1.6–7): this figure adds six years to the age paraded at the end of the first book of *Epistles* (see above) and a decade to that advertised (at least partly ironically) as already past the time of love in the second book of *Odes* (2.4.22–4). Accordingly, love and its sympotic context appear only in the sequence of poems 4.10–13 (see further below), while the rest of the book is dedicated to weightier themes. This change from the first collection is interestingly indexed in 4.7 and 4.8: 4.7, the famous ode to Torquatus, linking the return of spring with thoughts of changing seasons and human mortality, echoes that to Sestius in 1.4, but without the explicit sympotic and erotic references of the earlier poem (1.4.16–20), while 4.8, stressing the power of poetry to commemorate great deeds, uses the first Asclepiad metre reserved in the first collection for marking Horace's own poetic ambitions in 1.1 and 3.30 (see section 2B above), and apparently honours Censorinus for his military services to Rome.[37]

---

[36] For recent helpful material on the *Carmen* see Chapter V below.
[37] See Harrison 1990.

This turn to more nationalistic themes in Horace's final lyric book is partly thematized in 4.2.[38] There Horace addresses Iullus Antonius, claiming that it is impossible to imitate Pindar, the grandest of the Greek lyric poets, and encouraging Iullus in an alternative epic project to praise the victorious Augustus on his forthcoming return from German campaigns. Horace's strictures against Pindaric imitation are at least partly belied in this same poem, where Pindar's function as the encomiast of the victories of great leaders surely points to Horace's own celebrations of Augustus, as well in the Pindaric colour of 4.8[39] and the very obviously Pindaric victory odes for the two imperial princes Tiberius and his brother Drusus (4.4 and 4.14), which celebrate their conquests of the Raeti and Vindelici in 15 BCE. The framework of Pindaric celebration of athletic victory is here turned to the praise of Roman military success.

This nationalistic tendency of the book comes to a climax in 4.5 and 4.15, which address Augustus himself directly: 4.5 longs for his return to Italy and honours him as bringer of peace and prosperity,[40] while 4.15 rounds off Horace's lyric output with an equally enthusiastic encomium of the *princeps*.[41] In both these poems Horace moves into the first-person plural in his descriptions of the capacity of the Roman nation to praise its leader, suggesting solidarity with the community's feelings. This capacity to address and praise Augustus in a whole ode is a new feature in Horace's lyric output, no doubt expressing his increased personal and professional proximity to the *princeps*, but also matching the ability of Pindar to address the greatest figures of the Greek world: among the most enthusiastic political poems in the first collection, *Odes* 1.2 turns directly to Augustus only at the end (1.2.41–52), *Odes* 1.12 turns to Augustus at the end but actually addresses Jupiter (1.12.49–60), and *Odes* 3.5, though it suggests that Augustus will be a god on earth after his conquests, never addresses him personally.

The public and professional recognition conferred by the *Carmen saeculare* commission stimulates an important set of themes in *Odes* 4, which contains Horace's most extensive reflections so far on the status and function of the poet in Rome: the fame that the poet can

---

[38] See further Harrison 1995b.
[39] See further Harrison 1990.
[40] See DuQuesnay 1995.
[41] See Griffin 2002.

himself achieve is compared with athletic and military achievement (4.3.1–9), while the fame that he can confer on others is consistently seen as outlasting more conventional modes of commemoration (thematized in particular in the pair of poems 4.8 and 4.9). Horace's public fame is alluded to openly. In 4.3 he thanks the muse Melpomene for his celebrity (4.3.21–4), while in 4.6 he imagines his name recalled in later life by one of the maidens who had served in the choir at the *ludi saeculares* (4.6.41–4). This is the only self-naming by Horace by his *nomen gentilicium* (family name) in the *Odes* and one of only two in all his works (the other is at *Epist.* 1.14.5); it points to his high public recognition after 17 BCE.

This increasingly public aspect of Horace's poetic stance is a crucial feature of Book 4. At the same time, however, continuities with *Odes* 1–3 should not be neglected: this final lyric book coheres with as well as departs from the framework of the previous three. The sequence 4.10–13 is important here: 4.10 picks up the ironic address of 4.1 to Ligurinus and similarly looks to pederastic material in the earlier collection, while 4.11 is a sympotic/erotic ode celebrating the birthday of Maecenas. The appearance here both of this lighter material and of the great patron of *Odes* 1–3 again looks self-consciously back to the earlier collection in its themes. Meanwhile, 4.12 is another sympotic ode, addressed to a Vergilius with evident echoes of the *Eclogues* and *Aeneid*: though it is possible that a relative is meant rather than the poet himself, dead for some years by the time of the poem's publication, both addressee and theme look back to the first collection (where the poet Virgil was addressed in 1.3). Likewise, 4.13 returns not only to an erotic theme of the first collection (the beloved grown old, also alluded to in 4.10 – compare 1.25) but also to a name used for a love object in *Odes* 3.10, to which it serves as an ironic pendant (in 3.10 Lyce rejected Horace, and now she no longer attracts him).

But the main emphasis in *Odes* 4 is undoubtedly that on the mature poet at the zenith of his career, having established himself in a public and national role. One further feature allied to this is the prominence in the book of odes to addressees who are both young and from the highest level of Rome's elite – the imperial princes Tiberius and Drusus (4.4 and 4.14), Iullus Antonius, the nephew and then favourite of Augustus (4.2), and Paullus Fabius Maximus (4.1, which alludes to his recent marriage to Augustus' niece Marcia). As with his more direct relationship with Augustus himself (see above), Horace presents himself as operating at the very highest level in Rome, but the youth of

these addressees also allows him to come across as a fatherly figure dis-
pensing wise advice to the younger generation. This stance, natural to
the ageing poet, had been deployed with good effect with addressees
such as Lollius, Florus, Celsus, and Scaeva in the first book of
Epistles,[42] and will be seen as central to the last phase of Horace's career
in his return to *sermo*. The older poet who advises the younger literary
aspirant Iullus Antonius in *Odes* 4.2 is a recognizable anticipation of the
national authority on poetry in the didactic mode of the second book of
Epistles and the *Ars poetica*.

D. Epistles *2 and* Ars poetica: *final return to* sermo

As already mentioned, the three poems *Epistles* 2.1 and 2.2 and the *Ars
poetica*, which may have been conceived by the poet as a unit and poetic
book, seem to belong together in the final phase of Horace's poetic
career.[43] *Epistles* 2.1 and the *Ars poetica* can both be dated to the period
after *Odes* 4 and in particular to the period between 12 BCE and the
death of the poet in 8; though *Epistles* 2.2 is usually dated shortly
after the first book of *Epistles*, *c.*19 BCE, there are plausible arguments
for grouping it chronologically with *Epistles* 2.1 and the *Ars*. In particular, Florus' service under Tiberius, which opens both *Epistles* 2.2 and
Epistles 1.3, may refer to two different campaigns rather than the
same Eastern expedition: indeed, 2.2.1, *fidelis amice Neroni* ('loyal
friend to Nero') may allude pointedly to Florus' years of faithful service
since *Epistles* 1.3. Meanwhile, the references in *Epistles* 2.2 to having
given up writing lyric could be to the second 'lyric silence' after *Odes*
4 (13) rather than the gap between *Odes* 1–3 and the *Carmen saeculare*
(23–17 BCE) alluded to in *Epistles* 1.1 (see above).

   This sense of a final phase in a distinguished career is accentuated by
several features of these three poems as a group. First, all deal with the
theme of poetry in general from a didactic angle. *Epistles* 2.1, addressing
Augustus himself, argues against the automatic honouring of older writers, criticizes the crudity of early Roman literature, and praises the civ-
ilizing influence of literary Hellenism. *Epistles* 2.2, to Florus, himself
probably a poet, talks about the right and wrong ways to approach

---

[42] E.g. 1.4.19–20, 1.32.11–12, 3.20.5–16.
[43] See Harrison 2008, the arguments of which are summarized here, and have been accepted
e.g. by Nisbet 2007: 18; Günther 2013a: 48; and Rudd 2007. Similar views are stated independently in Holzberg 2009: 28–29.

the profession of poetry, using Horace himself as an example. Finally, the *Ars poetica* famously sets out a series of precepts on poetry, its kinds, and the behaviour of the poet for the appreciation of the young Pisones. This role of poetic preceptor follows naturally on the advisory role which Horace had assumed to some addressees in *Epistles* 1 and *Odes* 4 (see above).

Secondly, all three poems share a sense of Horace's self-location in the Roman literary tradition: a wide range of previous poets is discussed, and there is some emphasis on the now dead Virgil and Varius, suggesting that Horace has some consciousness that the great days of Augustan poetry are coming to an end and that he is the final survivor of the generation which emerged around the time of Actium (31 BCE). Thirdly, all three poems deal with the theme of the usefulness of the poet and of Horace in particular to the community of Rome (*Epist.* 2.1.124, 2.2.121; *Ars poetica* 396–401), though typically this self-elevation is on each occasion followed by some final self-deflation: *Epistles* 2.1 concludes with the lowly fate of bad poets and their verses which Horace seeks to avoid (2.1.267–70), *Epistles* 2.2 with a playful self-address which suggests that the poet has enjoyed more than enough of the pleasures of life (2.2.213–16), and the *Ars* with the celebrated picture of the mad poet who will not leave his listener alone (470–6).

Finally, and perhaps most tellingly, it is in these poems that Horace gives us the fullest retrospective on his poetic career, augmenting the account in *Epistles* 1.19 (see section 2B above). This is done through the poet's self-representation as the author of a body of works in various genres which can now be presented for comparison and assessment. In *Epistles* 2.2 Horace's friends are said to differ in their preferences between *Odes*, *Epodes*, and *sermones* (59–60), and this generic variety is matched at *Ars* 79–85, where Horace refers to Archilochean iambic invective and Pindaric lyric epinician. This last passage implicitly covers key elements of Horace's career with elegant indirection, moving from Archilochus (as the model of the *Epodes*) via a digression about the use of iambics in drama to a Pindarizing account of lyric, which clearly encapsulates the major themes of the *Odes*: hymns, epinicians (no doubt looking to the Pindaric imitations of *Odes* 4), love, and the symposium. Once again the element of surveying the poet's output, whether explicitly or implicitly, would be appropriate to a unified and self-consciously 'late' book in Horace's poetic career.

These factors, taken together, present a consistent picture of the poet in his fifties, a self-constructed Roman laureate at the end of a distinguished career, who combines proud self-elevation and self-inscription in the annals of literature with a beguiling touch of self-deprecation. In returning to *sermo* and his earliest and least ambitious literary mode, albeit in the refined epistolary form which he himself had created in the first book of *Epistles* and in a group of works including the longest poem in his output, Horace's poetic career has in a sense come full circle. Though the commitment and importance of his strictures on poetry are not to be underestimated, Horace here elects to bow out on a note of self-restraint and irony towards his own undoubtedly paramount poetic status, and to return to a modified form of the poetic mode in which he had made his name perhaps a quarter-century previously.

3 Self-presentation

The different poetic kinds which constitute Horace's output all seem to have been chosen in part because of the primacy of the poet's voice: Lucilian *sermo* with its strong 'autobiographical' element, Archilochean iambus with its 'personal' invective, Lesbian 'monodic' lyric with its prominent 'I', and epistolary *sermo* with its inevitably central letter-writer, further layered in the *Ars poetica* with the didactic voice of the instructor. Older critics used to regard the first-person voice in Horace as an unproblematic reporter of reality – indeed we can say that this biographical-realistic model was the reigning paradigm up to and beyond Fraenkel's *Horace* in 1957. Much recent work is more nuanced, arguing that any first-person Horatian statements are likely to have been influenced by rhetorical, social, and poetical strategies of various kinds,[44] and must be treated with suitable scepticism from the biographical perspective.[45] Discussions of the use of 'I' in the Greek lyric tradition which Horace uses in the *Odes* have yielded similar complexities,[46] as have discussions of the first-person voice in Roman satire for the *Satires*.[47] Critics used to be much concerned with *persona* theory, the idea that the poet puts on a mask and becomes a character in his own work;[48]

---

[44] Davis 1991; Oliensis 1998; McNeill 2001; Schmidt 2002b.
[45] See especially Horsfall 1998.
[46] See e.g. Lefkowitz 1991; Slings 1990.
[47] E.g. Muecke 2007.
[48] See e.g. Anderson 1982.

in a post-theoretical age, most scholars are well aware of the potential complexities of any first-person statement in literature.[49] In what follows I want to consider some aspects of the poet's self-representation in Horace's work, in particular the deliberate downplaying in his poetic texts of some of the most important events in his biographical life and his sometimes self-deprecating presentation of his poetic status.[50]

A. The protected poet

Apart from the brief information about his schooling (see section 1 above), we hear little of the young Horace except for one memorable anecdote at *Odes* 3.4.9–20, when the poet reports that he was miraculously covered with leaves by birds when lost in the country as a child. Scholars rightly point out that such myths of miraculous preservation in deadly perils of childhood (very real in the ancient world) belong especially to stories about poets,[51] and the reader may legitimately suspect that this episode may not be wholly autobiographical. Yet the traditional form and likely fictionality of the myth is carefully counterbalanced by the reality effect inherent in the minute details of Apulian landscape: the poet name-checks three local places (Acherontia, Bantia, and Forentum), the only time that the reader of Horace hears about the small communities of his home country. Thus we find a clear combination of fantasy and realism which avoids spilling over into one or the other.

A similar technique seems to be operating in the famous encounter with the wolf at *Odes* 1.22.9–16, where the poet claims to have frightened off a wolf from his Sabine farm by singing love poetry. Once again, we may doubt whether such an encounter actually occurred: as commentators observe, the love-struck Horace here enjoys the freedom from harm traditional for lovers, and one might add that the poet is depicted as an amusing anti-Orpheus (wild animals flee his music instead of flocking to it). But once again an element of fantasy is combined with an element of detailed realism: the incident is carefully located on Horace's Sabine estate or indeed in the wilds near it.

[49] See e.g. Mayer 2003.
[50] Here I draw on Harrison 2007d.
[51] See e.g. Horsfall 1998: 46.

A similar lack of clarity can be found concerning another reported incident in Horace's life, his escape from a falling tree. In the continued 'autobiography' of *Odes* 3.4, Horace names this among the three great perils of his life (3.4.25–8), while in *Odes* 2.17 it is seen as the greatest of them, from which he was saved by Faunus and the protection of Mercury, bringing in another deity whose patronage is claimed more than once (see below) for the poet (2.17.27–30). In *Odes* 3.8, on the occasion of the Matronalia which seems to have coincided with the time of the incident (early March), he offers an annual sacrifice of thanksgiving for his deliverance, while in *Odes* 2.13 a whole poem is devoted to a curse on the tree and to imagining the trip to the Underworld so narrowly avoided. It is hard to believe that the incident is wholly fictional, and the fact that it is not mentioned in the more sober autobiographical details found in the *Satires* and *Epodes* might suggest that it took place after 30 BCE; yet the poems offer no fixed date and location for such an important event, a gap which scholars have vainly sought to fill.[52] The symbolic point of the incident – the divine preservation of the protected poet – is clearly more important than its actual place in Horace's life.

B. *The poet at war: Philippi, Naulochus, and Actium*

As already noted (see section 1 above), Horace fought at Philippi in 42 BCE with Brutus against the future Augustus, a record which he does not attempt to conceal in his poetry (see *Sat.* 1.6.48, 1.7; *Odes* 2.7; *Odes* 3.14.37–8; *Epist.* 2.2.46–8), though flattering mention is usually made of the righteous might of the other side.[53] The main account of the battle is to be found in *Odes* 2.7, judiciously framed as a welcome for a former comrade returning to Italy via a post-Actium amnesty (2.7.9–14). Here, as commentators have noted, Horace gives a brief and almost mythological account of the battle, and the stress is not on his command of a legion (cf. *Sat.* 1.6.48) but on his loss of his shield, which recalls the similar losses suffered by Archilochus and Alcaeus, two of Horace's poetic models, while his protector is Mercury, god of poetry, removing him from the battle in a magic mist like a Homeric hero. Thus Horace's role in a crucial military

---

[52] See especially Schmidt 2002b: 180–1, who dates the tree-fall to 33 BCE.
[53] See especially Horsfall 1998: 46.

event is seen through a symbolic and poetic perspective, and we are little wiser about what really happened. The choice of such a fantastic and poetic treatment also avoids the brutal details of the Philippi campaign in which thousands perished on both sides.[54]

In the list of Horace's three main life-dangers in *Odes* 3.4, mentioned above, the falling tree and Philippi are followed by a Sicilian incident, an apparent episode of near-drowning in 'the Sicilian wave' (3.4.25–8). It seems likely that it belongs to the period of the war against Sextus Pompeius and perhaps to the young Caesar's final and successful campaign of Naulochus (36 BCE.). The non-mention in Book 1 of the *Satires* of any connection with Naulochus is unproblematic, since that book is remarkably reticent about the political situation of the time. But, once again, an event which was clearly crucial in Horace's life and perhaps significant in his recently established position as *amicus* of Maecenas (Maecenas was at Naulochus, and Horace may well have accompanied him) is recorded in his poetry with tantalizing obscurity.

Whether Horace accompanied Maecenas to Actium, on which his poetry gives much more evidence, has been a question much debated by scholars.[55] In the *Epodes*, published soon after the battle and written with the hindsight of Caesarian victory, Horace begins his poetry book with a promise to attend his patron to the battle, and adds to this in the book's central poem what looks like a first-hand report of the battle, both of which strongly suggest that the poet was present with Maecenas. On the other hand, *Odes* 1.37 is cast as a celebration from Rome of the victory at Actium, the capture of Alexandria, and the suicide of Cleopatra: like Philippi in *Odes* 2.7, the battle is barely described, and there is no hint of autopsy. Of course, it is more than likely that Horace returned to Italy after Actium and did not go on to the Alexandrian campaign which concluded nine months later (the two are conflated in the ode), but it is surprising that he does not hint at his presence for at least part of the military proceedings which he describes. The poetic need for a schematic account of the battle, and the concentration on the end of Cleopatra, here elides any overtly autobiographical reminiscence.

---

[54] See Citroni 2001.
[55] Fraenkel 1957 held that both Maecenas and Horace were at Rome during Actium, but most scholars now place both Maecenas and Horace at Actium – see e.g. DuQuesnay 2002; Watson 2003: 57; Nisbet: 2007; 11–12; Günther 2013a. Anderson 2010:40 is still sceptical.

C. Poet and patron: estates and rewards

Maecenas' gift to Horace of the Sabine estate (mentioned in section 1 above) gave him both financial independence and access to the relaxed rural life which he so often desiderates in his work. But, as already noted, this event is nowhere directly recorded in the poems, and indirect allusions are so vague that an argument has been made that Horace was never given the farm but bought it himself independently, albeit with wealth derived from his connections with Maecenas.[56] At *Satires* 2.6.1–5 the poet expresses gratitude for an estate and incredulity that it is now his property, but does not thank Maecenas, who is not even addressed in the poem (though his friendship for the poet is strongly emphasized in 2.6.30–58). And though allusions to the Sabine estate and its wine are common in odes to Maecenas and can easily be interpreted as elegantly understated thanks (*Odes* 1.9.7, 1.20.1; cf. 3.1.47, 3.4.22), the two further passages which refer to the Sabine estate could easily be taken as general or noncommittal. *Epodes* 1.25–32, addressed to Maecenas, implies that Horace is a landowner and says *satis superque me benignitas tua / ditauit*, 'enough and more than enough has your kindness enriched me'. Meanwhile *Odes* 2.18.12–14, not addressed to Maecenas, again makes the point (without direct reference to Maecenas) that Horace needs no more than he has been given already – *nec potentem amicum / largiora flagito, / satis beatus unicis Sabinis*, 'nor do I ask my powerful friend for greater largesse, rich enough with my single Sabine estate'. Again the comparative *largiora* suggests that the rich friend has already shown generosity in the form of the Sabine estate, and the rich friend is surely Maecenas, but again the overall impression is vague and generalized. As mentioned earlier, Horace's indirect approach to acknowledging the gift of the Sabine estate not only shows delicacy towards Maecenas but also serves to conceal the crudely material workings of the client–patron relationship.[57]

D. The poet's fame: immortality and self-deprecation

The poet's future fame is a common topic of self-presentation in the poetry of Horace's middle and later periods (the *Odes* and *Epistles*).

---

[56] Bradshaw 1989.
[57] See Bowditch 2001, 2010.

In Book 4 of the *Odes* this topic seems especially serious, perhaps owing to the conscious closure of a poetic career and consequent concern with commemoration (see section 2C above). In *Odes* 1–3 and the first book of *Epistles*, however, the poet rarely treats this theme without some form of concomitant self-deprecation, one of his most attractive self-presenting strategies.

The future fame of the poet is immediately faced in the opening *Ode* (1.1.29–36). There, the proud boast of divine fellowship and of the patronage of the Muses and the ambition to become a member of the classic canon of lyric poets are lofty ideas, but all are punctured by the sting in the tail: the poet will strike the stars with his head (*sublimi feriam sidera uertice*), an incongruously literal picture which suggests a nasty headache. As we shall see, the deflation of grand claims is a topic of these Horatian self-promotions.

Similarly two-edged is the famous picture of Horace as a swan in the final poem of Book 2 of the *Odes*. Once again air travel is at issue, and the poet begins by presenting himself as in future metamorphosing into a grand poetic bird, soaring immortal above earthly trivialities through the fame of his poetry (2.20.1–8). But then, in the two central stanzas of the poem, this elevated picture is again deflated (2.20.9–16): the poetic swan here becomes jarringly literal, with strong focus on the physical details of the process of metamorphosis (rough skin, white hair, and feathered fingers and shoulders). It also pursues a dubious flight path: comparing oneself to Icarus (as he does) is not a recipe for a safe flight (as Horace notes at *Odes* 4.2.1–4), and this perhaps doomed swan will fly not to pleasant climes but to the ship-grave of the Bosphorus, the deserts of Africa, and the sterile tundra of Scythia. This is worldwide fame only of a sort; these virtually uninhabited regions are not cultured places or appreciative locales for poetry. Once again, immortality is rendered comical.

A similar approach can be seen in *Odes* 3.30, the mirror poem to 1.1 and in the same metre, and the seal poem of the first collection of *Odes*. This begins, like 2.20, with broad claims about immortality: Horace's poetic monument will be more durable than the Pyramids and last as long as Roman culture itself. But then the poem turns to more local ideas (3.30.10–14). There Horace names the river and mythical king of his own birthplace: his career and rise will be famous in his minor home region, a neat inversion of the common *topos* that a poet's work will make his marginal home city well known, comically suggesting that he will be appreciated (only?) in the backwoods by local fans. Yet again, grand claims are undermined by humour.

The last in this sequence of self-deprecations occurs in the seal poem to *Epistles* 1. There the poetry book of epistles is comically compared to a slave-boy to be prostituted/sold in the market. It (the boy/book) will lose popularity at Rome and then be exported to the provinces for less discriminating use (1.20.10–13). Here we can see a comic version of the worldwide fame of *Odes* 2.20: the boy/book goes not to glamorous and romantic locations but as a runaway slave or chain-gang member to two marginal developing towns of North Africa and Spain, both growing under Augustus. Finally, the boy/book will be called on to describe its author to potential buyers (1.20.19–28) – the poet was 'born of a freedman father' and in straitened circumstances 'stretched his wings wider than his nest', and was born in the year of Lollius' consulship. Here, in the more relaxed environment of the *Epistles*, we find clear ironization of the grander claims of the *Odes* about its author: the wings too large for the nest surely pick up and play with the poetic swan of *Odes* 2.20, and the stress on Horace's actual age and birthday is an undermining of lyric claims of immortality – he is a real and ephemeral person who fits the traditional framework of Roman consular dating. The date formula which ends Horace's epistle book amusingly echoes the kind of dating which begins the books of an annalistic Roman history, suggesting perhaps that the first book of *Epistles* is a kind of comic chronicle of his life at Rome.

III EARLY WORKS: *SATIRES* 1 AND 2, *EPODES*

1. Introduction

This first phase of Horace's poetic career has aroused extensive interest in recent scholarship, which has moved beyond the traditional teleological idea (crystallized by Fraenkel and others) that the *Satires* and *Epodes* are early experimental works in which the poet had not yet reached his highest level, to be achieved in the mature lyric glories of the *Odes* and the sage reflections of the *Epistles*.[1] This is a crucial period in Horace's career, and some key features emerge which will be central for his poetry. In this chapter I will look at the two books of *Satires* and that of the *Epodes*, considering each collection in turn, with a focus on important issues and scholarship.

2. *Satires* 1

Satires 1, once considered a rough-hewn work, has been rightly re-evaluated since Fraenkel. The most important event here has been the recent publication of the splendid commentary by Gowers (2012), the culmination of years of work on the book, which combines subtle and nuanced literary interpretation with impressive knowledge of the scholarly literature. Labate 1981 and Brown 1993 had been a considerable help in wrestling with these difficult poems, but Gowers' book now enables readers to appreciate their full subtle complexity in a style which is both approachable and witty. Also extensive and interesting is the Italian running commentary on both books by Fedeli (1994).

As one looks back, Rudd 1966, the first book to treat the *Satires* as an ambitious literary work, is still important nearly half a century on: it provides a sympathetic close reading of all the poems with a fine eye to literary texture and interaction, effectively grouping poems on similar themes together, and includes a key chapter on the proper names. Horace's works were also involved in the debates on persona theory

---

[1] There is no extensive treatment of the first phase of Horace's literary career to match that of Becker 1963 on his last, but Griffin 1993 provides some useful indications.

in the 1960s and 1970s, considering the potential gap between the first-person satirist and the author (see Chapter II above), with the most important material being gathered in the collected essays of Anderson (1982); a latter-day advocate, viewing the speaker of *Satires* 1.1–3 as a comic parody of an Epicurean street-philosopher, is Turpin 1998. Important here and elsewhere is the work of Freudenburg (1993), which takes a close look at the literary affinities and theoretical position of satire as practised by Horace, making instructive links with the tradition of ancient popular comedy, Hellenistic moralizing, and Roman literary and stylistic theory in analysing the sophisticated characterization of the poet's voice and self-presentation; links with Greek and Roman comedy have also been investigated by Delignon 2006. Most recently, Sharland 2010 sees *Satires* 1.1–3 as a collection of comic scenes where humour is generated by a self-satirizing speaker, usefully applying the Bakhtinian idea of polyphony in identifying these apparent monologues as dialogues. A substantial and interesting survey of both books of *Satires* is also offered in Courtney 2013b.

An influential analysis of Book 1 in particular is Zetzel 1980, which not only presents *Satires* 1 as a well-ordered poetry book influenced by the recent *Eclogues* of Horace's friend Virgil (on the careful order of Book 1 [and Book 2 as well] see also Knorr 2004) but also points to the complex self-revelation of the poet yielded by a linear reading, moving through the voices of street moralist, literary critic, and former supporter of Brutus to acceptance as a part of the new Caesarian regime via Maecenas. Gowers 2003, following a similar line, persuasively argues that this first book appropriately presents various crucial 'narratives of emergence' – becoming a poet, leaving his humble home and family, escaping from Philippi, joining Maecenas – often via indirect and metaphorical means, and focuses on the idea of development and civilization. This focus on indirection is shared by Schlegel 2005, who argues that in *Satires* 1 Horace 'presents the bite but does not do the biting',[2] skilfully combining a mild and moderate tone with an awareness both of the danger of alienating the reader through excessive aggression and of the fundamental issues of power and speech with which satire is concerned. Another interesting analysis of the

---

[2] Schlegel 2005: 6.

book is Gowers 2009, which points to its concern with ends and closure of all kinds.

A clear issue in *Satires* 1 is that of Horace's political position. Moving from the status of a defeated Republican to that of a Maecenas-sponsored poet might be thought to imply some kind of commitment to the new Caesarian regime, but the surface of the book has relatively little to say on the issue, and until recently scholars in general thought of the *Satires* as non-political. DuQuesnay 1984 is important in alerting readers to political elements, arguing that *Satires* 1 implicitly supports Maecenas and the young Caesar, and suggesting specific evidence of anti-Pompeian factionalism: 38–35 BCE, the likely period of composition of the *Satires*, is also the period of renewed civil war in south Italy, the Bellum Siculum, concluded in effect by the defeat of Sextus Pompeius at Naulochus in September 36 and his subsequent death. *Satires* 1 contains no overt attack on Sextus and little on his supporters; there is one laudatory allusion (1.3.4–6) to the young Augustus and Julius Caesar, but no mention of the former's victory or military campaigns. However, Horace's loyalty to Maecenas, a prominent theme of the book, can be seen as a platform for indirect demonstration of Caesarian loyalties: the emphasis in 1.5, the famous journey to Brundisium, is on the poet's amusing experiences, with the major political purpose (accompanying Maecenas and others on a top-level diplomatic mission for Caesar to Antony) very much in the background. The detailed triviality of the poem contrasts with its weighty political context; Horace shows that he is on the inside without revealing any political details, thus demonstrating both loyalty and discretion. In particular, the verbal battle between Sarmentus and Messius could present a comic version of the distrust and potential hostilities (as we know retrospectively) between Caesar and Antony in 37:[3] the quarrels of triumvirs are reduced to pleasant dinnertime entertainment (70), and the other minor disasters of the journey are amusing versions of further battles avoided. Even the Epicurean theology of 101–3 may suggest peace between the great.

Equally subtle is 1.7, which seems to show (like *Odes* 2.7) that the poet can write with allusion to his Republican past in a book addressed to Maecenas, though significantly he does not present this supposed comic episode from Brutus' campaigns in Asia as the eye-witness

---

[3] See Pelling 1996: 25–6.

account it could be, and never makes it clear whether he was himself present.[4] The joke on tyrannicide to which the poem builds up is made against Brutus, and it has been argued that the poem presents him as a tyrant himself and represents a clear attack on the poet's previous political loyalties.[5] However, Brutus is described as a properly constituted magistrate in Asia (*Bruto praetore*, 1.7.18), and appears in the poem only as spectator and addressee of the low-life invective competition between Rupilius Rex and Persius. Equally, it has been suggested that Brutus as supreme commander with the power of life and death looks forward subtly and subversively to the young Caesar himself.[6] One could add that this poem presents Republican squabbling in a suitably comic form, followed by comic Caesarian order in 1.8 with Priapus expelling witches from the Esquiline to engender the peace of Maecenas' own famous *horti* (1.8.14–16): no doubt it was Maecenas who set up the watchman statue of Priapus, who repeats on the comic and dramatic level the clearance work of his master.

Similarly, the poem in which the poet narrates how he linked up with Maecenas is nicely ambiguous (1.6). Neatly placed after a poem in which Horace is clearly on the inside, we have another about how he got there, through personal worth and despite his dubious family background. This poem carefully uses Maecenas' public quietism to draw a parallel between the select Callimachean poet and the socially select Maecenas, presenting them as naturally suited to each other. The hard social and political realities are obscured: there is no mention of the poet's (potentially politically useful) poetry, surely the reason why Virgil and Varius introduced him to Maecenas (1.6.55), and none of Maecenas' political importance, though, as DuQuesnay (1984) points out, the nine-month gap between his first meeting with the poet and their second encounter (61) is probably due to another high-level diplomatic mission in autumn 38 (see Appian *B Civ.* 5.92). Again discretion rules.

This poem finds its opposite in 1.9, where the poet is famously accosted by a pest in the streets of Rome. His unwelcome companion has social and (non-Callimachean) literary ambitions (1.9.7, 23), and wants acquaintance with Maecenas (1.9.43); he wants the poet to introduce him, just as Horace was himself introduced in 1.6, and the poem

---

[4] See Gowers 2002.
[5] DuQuesnay 1984.
[6] Henderson 1998: 73–107.

is full of uncomfortable intimations that the pest is a dark version of Horace himself, a literary man on the make seeking the favour of Maecenas,[7] as well as suggesting that the pest goes about his business in the wrong way. The poet politely rejects him and presents Maecenas, as in 1.6, as a virtuous chooser of virtuous friends, not to be hurried or forced (1.9.44–57); but this high-minded account of friendship is brilliantly undercut by another (non-Maecenas?) friend, Fuscus (cf. *Odes* 1.22; *Ep.* 1.10), who shows the mischievous side of friendship in refusing to rescue the poet from the pest. Finally, however, the putative interloper fails, and gets his due comeuppance (74–8). Once again, discretion is maintained and potential political elements suppressed.

Various studies have led to a greater understanding of individual poems in the book. Already mentioned are Henderson's typically challenging analyses of 1.7 and 1.9, and 1.5 has also received particular attention.[8] Gowers' article gives a nicely nuanced linear reading of Horace's journey poem and its skilful manipulation of the reader's sense of direction and expectations in both time and space. She also alludes to its imitation of the *Odyssey*, pursued to a greater degree by both Cuchiarelli and Harrison: the journey out to Brundisium clearly echoes and inverts Odysseus' journey home to Ithaca, and Horace is in a sense returning to his native country, travelling through the familiar mountain landscape of Apulia (1.5.77–8) and passing not far from his home town of Venusia.

In particular, the speaker's first-person narrative of his own journey recalls and reworks Odysseus' narrative of his travels to Alcinous in *Odyssey* 9–12, often by inversion and contrast, as might be expected in the modification of an epic original for a satiric context. Like Odysseus in the *Odyssey*, Horace sets off from a great city, Rome, the historical successor of Odysseus' Troy. The main narrative incident of the poem – the battle of wits at Cocceius' house between two low-life characters – recalls the famous parasitic battle of the *Odyssey*, between the beggar Irus and the disguised Odysseus in *Odyssey* 18, which involves a considerable amount of repartee as well as blows, an Odyssean connection underlined by Sarmentus' insulting comparison of Messius to the Cyclops (1.5.63). Likewise, when Horace sees smoke rising from a villa near his home territory (1.5.80), this surely

---

[7] Henderson 1999: 202–27.
[8] E.g. Gowers 1993a; Cucchiarelli 2001:15–55; Harrison 2007b: 86–93.

recalls Odysseus' yearning to see the smoke of his own land (*Od.* 1.58), and the poet's complete failure to get anywhere with the girl whom he finds at his stopping place contrasts amusingly with Odysseus' apparent tendency to find a complaisant girl in every port. Cucchiarelli adds to these epic undertones echoes of the low worlds of Greek comedy and iambic (pointing nicely to the Aristophanic frogs of 1.5.14 and the element of the *Frogs* in the contest of abuse), indicating a programmatic statement about the centrality of comedy for Horatian *sermo* (which parallels the evocation of Aristophanes at the start of 1.4 and the programmatic *ridentem dicere uerum* ['to tell the truth with laughter'] of 1.1.24).

Recent scholarship clearly attaches increased importance to the book's intertextuality.[9] Added to the Homeric elements already noted is increased awareness of links with Callimachus in R. Scodel 1987; the crucial links with Lucilius await an updated version of the still-useful Fiske 1920, though some stimulating points are made by Freudenburg 2001: 15–55. Lucretius' status as recent expositor of Greek philosophy in Latin hexameter verse has been underestimated in analysis of the *Satires*, not least because he is unmentioned in Horace's poems.[10] A number of important Lucretian passages (among other literary allusions) are echoed in *Satires* 1, not least in the programmatic 1.1, which begins with the Lucretian *qui fit ... ut?* ('how does it happen that ...?'; cf. Lucretius 4.877, 5.904), picks up in its image of giving cakes to boys to induce learning (1.1.24–6) the key image of giving them honey with their medicine (Lucretius 1.936–47 = 4.11–22), and in its closing picture of the man who leaves life like a sated dinner guest (1.1.117–21) looks to the same image at Lucretius 3.938 and 3.960. In 1.3.38–40 allusion is made to the well-known tendency of lovers to ignore the beloved's physical faults or even to turn them into enhancements, picking up Lucretius 4.1150–6, where the poet suggests that the reader makes his own problems in this respect; in the same poem, the description of primitive man (1.3.99–112) clearly points to the famous exposition of the same topic in Lucretius 5. In each case the Lucretian material is suitably modified for its new generic location in the lower and more brutal world of satire. In general, modern scholarship is more sharply aware of the creative element in the contact between satire and

---

[9] For an effective summary, see Gowers 2012: 22–4.
[10] See Freudenburg 1993: 19.

other poetic genres, whether notionally higher hexameter works or poems in lower literary kinds such as epigram, not to forget prose genres such as historiography.[11]

3. *Satires* 2

The interpretation of this book is now much eased by Muecke 1993, which provides a useful parallel translation of these difficult poems, and also a commentary which gives details beyond the usual scope of its modestly framed series. All readers of *Satires* 2 now need access to this volume (alongside the Italian running commentary of Fedeli 1994). We await the commentary of Freudenburg for the Cambridge Greek and Latin Classics series.

The move of the second book of Horace's *Satires* into a world where the poet-satirist takes a back seat and listens to a number of interlocutors has not always been appreciated, though its links with the narrative frameworks of Plato's dialogues were well picked up by Fraenkel. In more recent work, scholars with a more sophisticated approach to narrative voice have relished the complexities which the poet's choice generates. The book's dialogic aspect has been interestingly explored by Sharland 2010, appropriately using Bakhtinian ideas of the carnivalesque to analyse the two Saturnalian conversations in 2.3 and 2.7, and exploring the complex texture of these poems and 2.2 through the Bakhtinian notion of heteroglossia, the insertion of other voices. Oliensis 1998 has suggested that self-incrimination is a key theme for the book, not only in the commonly accepted idea that its speakers condemn themselves through Horatian irony but also in the notion that these new speakers are, in fact, uncomfortably like the poet-speaker of the first book of the *Satires*.

Harrison 2013a has explored this latter idea in more detail: in 2.2 the speaker Ofellus can be seen as resembling the poet in eclectic philosophical interests (2.2.3), in suffering from the land confiscations (2.2.127–36), and in advocating the simple country life (cf. 2.6), while in 2.3 Damasippus recalls the Horace of Book 1 in losing his property (2.3.18–20), and belongs to the bustling commercial world which Horace might have entered himself in the footsteps of his father

---

[11] For details on Horatian interaction in the *Satires* with poetic genres, see Harrison 2007b: 75–103; on interaction with historiography, see Woodman 2009.

(cf. 1.6.85–7). Like the Horace of the first book, the speaker is concerned to summarize and retail the views of other philosophers (2.3.34), and uses an Aesopic fable to make a moral point (2.3.314–20; cf. e.g. 2.6.79–117). At the beginning of the poem, Horace asks *sed unde / tam bene me nosti?* ('but how did you get to know me so well?'). Damasippus replies that since his business failure he has had time to concentrate on the doings of others, but the question might also suggest that he (like Ofellus) is a second Horace. Similarly, the Catius of 2.4 explores (albeit *ad absurdum*) Horace's weakness for food (2.7.29–35), while the Odysseus of 2.5 is another character who has lost his property and needs to start again from the bottom, and recalls the poet's self-characterization as a comic Odysseus in 1.5, the Journey to Brundisium (see section 1 above).

The book's characters, as well as its speakers, can reflect aspects of the satirist's self-representation. This can be clearly seen in its most famous poem, 2.6.[12] This Platonic-style symposiastic dialogue is the stage for the famous Aesopic-style fable of the town and country mouse (2.6.79–117), in which the country mouse tries the fleshpots and dangers of the city with his urban relative but is only too glad to return to the country. The tale is told in the voice of Cervius, a rustic neighbour, another embedded character voice, but the technique of using a moralizing fable recalls the voice of the poet (see above, on 2.3). The country mouse has often been seen as an analogue for Horace, keen to withdraw to the country and avoid the pressures of city life which he has described earlier in the poem. However, the town mouse is also recognizably Horatian: his facile Epicurean address to the country mouse comically reflects the sympotic exhortations of *carpe diem* in the *Odes* (2.6.93–7), and the poem in fact presents the cultural and social complexities of Horace's life as a poet: his poetry is often written in the country (2.3.11–12, 2.6.16–17), but that country location is itself a gift from the urban Maecenas, and the subject of his satire is largely urban vice. Horace can never be only the country mouse; he must be the town mouse too.

Satires 2.1 has continued to attract attention concerning the issue of Roman satire and the law: the question of how far the satirist can go has been seen as both a reaction to some of the more aggressive attacks of Book 1 and also a reflection of the contemporary Roman environment.[13]

---

[12] For recent contributions to its study see Oliensis 1998: 46–51; Bowditch 2001:142–54; Cucchiarelli 2001: 162–8.

Satires 2.8, the *cena Nasidieni,* placed in its climactic position, has been increasingly seen as programmatic and metapoetic, following the important interpretation by Gowers 1993b, a book which crucially brings to the fore the literary symbolism of food for satire in general.[14] Most recently, Sharland 2011 argues that *Satires* 2.8 reviews and reflects on not only much of Horace's prior writing but also the preceding ten to fifteen years of civil war, and that some of its figures bear traces of the past, including the recently deceased Cleopatra.

4. *Epodes*

Once again, the emergence of modern commentaries in the last two decades has been a crucial element in advancing the study of these sometimes difficult and often neglected poems; their invective and obscene content, previously something of a barrier to exegesis, can now be openly analysed in a more relaxed era. No fewer than three commentaries have appeared: Cavarzere 1992, stimulating and scholarly beyond the format of its series; Mankin 1995, an effective and reliable guide (if a little austere) and an important advance in incorporating modern views on ancient Greek iambos as not simply autobiographical (thus providing an important starting point for Horace's carefully constructed persona); and Watson 2003, a massive and long-awaited volume. Watson's commentary is splendid on historical context, *Realien,* and relevant literary models; its initial interpretative essays on each poem could be considered relatively conservative in comparison with other modern work, but are well balanced and thoroughly aware of all the bibliography. This is a volume which will last for several decades as a standard tool of research.

As already noted, the modern study of these poems has benefitted from the recent reassessment of the archaic Greek iambic tradition of Archilochus and Hipponax, as well as of Callimachus' Hellenistic *Iambi.*[15] These connections can be seen in the papers collected in Cavarzere et al. 2001, which in effect surveys the whole Greek (and earlier Roman) iambic corpus, and contains two papers on the *Epodes* (Barchiesi 2001b and Harrison 2001b) which set out to show how

---

[13] See Muecke 1995; McGinn 2001.

[14] Along these lines, see also Freudenburg 1995; Caston 1997; Marchesi 2005.

[15] On the latter's links with the *Epodes,* see especially Heyworth 1993.

Horace modifies the Greek tradition, creating a dialogue with his models and transforming them for the new literary and cultural context of Rome in the 30s BCE. Many have suggested that, as in the case of toning down the aggression of Lucilius in the *Satires*, the poet's self-presentation in the *Epodes* deliberately tempers the invective of Archilochus, whether they connect this with the poet's general moderation or with the idea that he is somehow impotent.[16]

The generic diversity which used to provide a problem for the book's interpretation has now become a focus of particular interest and evidence of both its well-wrought literary texture and its awareness of literary history. Important here is the already mentioned link with the *Iambi* of Callimachus, with its evident generic variety, where (for example) themes from epigram and lyric epinician are found in iambic form (*Iambi* 7, 8, and 9), and where at least one poem (*Iambus* 13) is explicitly devoted to the discussion of multiple poetic genres. The *Epode* book plainly followed its Callimachean predecessor in this feature of generic interaction: recent work has shown contact between the rural colouring of *Epode* 2 and Virgil's *Eclogues* and *Georgics* (the latter surely known to Horace before publication), between *Epodes* 11 and 15 and contemporary love elegy, between *Epodes* 13 and 14 and Horace's own incipient *Odes*, and between *Epode* 16, Greek civic elegy, and hexameter prophecy.[17] A running issue is the clear link between *Epode* 16 and *Eclogue* 4, both of which incorporate prophecies about the future of Rome expressed in shared bucolic features: the balance of opinion now seems to be that the pessimistic Horatian poem responds to its optimistic Virgilian predecessor, perhaps as a reaction to political developments.[18]

This last point evokes another aspect of the *Epodes* which has received much attention in recent scholarship: its links with history and particularly with the battle of Actium. Most readers of *Epodes* 1 and 9 now conclude that these poems suggest that Horace was present at Actium, doubted by Fraenkel and others: the prominent promise to accompany Maecenas there in *Epode* 1 would look strange after the battle had it not been fulfilled, and the evidence of *Epode* 9

---

[16] Watson 1995. The possible phallic pun on the poet's name 'floppy' at 15.12, *nam si quid in Flacco uiri est* ('if there is anything of a man in Flaccus/floppy'), has been popular here: see Fitzgerald 1988; Oliensis 1991; contested by Watson 2003.

[17] See the details in Watson 2003 and elaborations in Harrison 2007b.

[18] See Watson 2003: 486–8; Harrison 2007b: 132–4.

does seem to suggest autopsy of the battle.[19] Another similar issue is that of the putative historical context of *Epodes* 7 and 16, which seem to belong to a time well before Actium, but refer openly to civil war (unlike *Epode* 9, where the foreign nature of the adversary is stressed, following Caesarian spin) and express pessimism about the future.[20] The most persuasive explanation has been that of Nisbet 1984, who argues that these are early poems expressing views about the renewed outbreak of civil war in 38 BCE against Sextus Pompeius, and who neatly suggests that they stimulated Maecenas' interest in Horace about the same time, described in *Satires* 1.6 (see above). Like the *Satires* and Virgil's *Eclogues*, the *Epodes* would then bear traces of the poet's views and loyalties changing over time, and some evidence of the protest poetry which might have alerted political powers to make use of a new literary voice.

Another issue which has come to the fore in the last generation is that of the book's structure, following a general tendency in the criticism of Latin poetry. Carrubba 1969, Schmidt 1977, and Dettmer 1983 have given useful views of the question, and commentators in particular have been interested in the effect both of a sequential reading of the structure and of a detached view. In the latter, the centrality of *Epode* 9 is clear, again reflecting a modern interest in the middles of poetic books,[21] and also the ring-compositional balance of the opening and closing poems. Metrically, there is a clear development between the epodic ('echoing' long and short) couplets of *Epodes* 1–10, and the mixture of dactylic and iambic metres in 11–16, with the final poem, 17, giving the first appearance of stichic (continuous) iambics. Though most of the metrical combinations found in the *Epodes* are now known to be Archilochean,[22] the increasing incidence of dactylic elements in *Epodes* 11–16 (as well as their content) seems to suggest more interaction with contemporary hexameter genres such as pastoral, oracle, and love elegy.[23]

One aspect of the *Epode* book which modern scholars have found particularly difficult is that of the two poems which viciously attack women for their ageing bodies and consequent incapacity to attract

---

[19] See above, Chapter 2, n. 55.
[20] See Ableitinger-Grünberger 1971.
[21] E.g. Kyriakidis and Di Martino 2004.
[22] See Watson 2003: 43–5.
[23] Harrison 2007b: 104–35.

the poet sexually (*Epodes* 8 and 12). Earlier scholars and translators were troubled by these because of their obscene content; more recently, in a post-feminist world, many have found it hard to deal with the objectification of the female body which these poems represent, and it is difficult to disagree with the view that they represent an unattractive assertion of aggressive masculinity, even if they stand in a long-established literary tradition.[24] Another female figure who has received particular attention is Canidia, who has been seen as the 'dark muse' of the book and a symbol of civil war parallel to Cleopatra;[25] attempts to connect her name with Antony's supporter Canidius[26] are perhaps less attractive than its destructive link with the devastating dog star.[27] Canidia's role as witch and her magic rituals have been investigated in great detail by Watson in his commentary on *Epodes* 5 and 17;[28] the fact that she stars in the two longest poems and is a creator of *carmina* (meaning both 'poems' and 'spells') has suggested to some that she represents the dark side of Horace himself.[29]

The most recent full-length account of the *Epodes* is T. Johnson 2012, the only major literary-critical volume on the work in the last generation. Johnson reacts interestingly against the common emphasis on Horace's impotence and weakness in the book, arguing that Horace's iambic poetics are characterized by the pattern 'transgression–responsion–fusion': conventional boundaries are crossed in the abuse and aggression of invective, which then elicits an opposing response, presented in opposing characters or discourse; this creates a community in which reciprocal positions can come together, thus making iambic aggression a unifying influence. Johnson evokes the ritual and festival elements in the Greek iambic tradition to suggest that iambos for Horace, too, can have positive social and poetic results. This tunes in both with the emphasis in modern scholarship on the creative diversity of literary form in Horace's book (see above) and with the political placement of the *Epodes* as a kind of carnivalesque celebration in a post-Actium era. It is a challenging new interpretation to which the next generation of critics will need to respond.

---

[24] See Grassmann 1966; Richlin 1992: 109–13; Henderson 1999: 173–201.
[25] Fitzgerald 1988; Oliensis 1991, 1998: 64–101.
[26] Nisbet 1984.
[27] Oliensis 1991.
[28] Watson 2003.
[29] Oliensis 1998: 64–101.

5. Conclusion

In the last generation, both the *Satires* and the *Epodes* have emerged from a period of critical neglect, a neglect which was due to a number of cultural factors: the view that these are early and difficult experiments on the way to the 'real' Horace; a concern with their sometimes obscene and rebarbative subject matter, which made them unsuitable for study by the young; a lack of understanding of their literary models and context; and a consequent lack of the kind of detailed scholarship which has always existed for Horace's more mature works. The next generation now has a full range of fundamental scholarly aids and nuanced literary criticism with which to work, and we should expect a period of stimulating output. Key Horatian features (linguistic and stylistic specificity and polish, complex presentation of the first-person poet, intricate intertextuality, and interaction with other literary genres) are plainly present, and set a pattern for future work.

IV MIDDLE PERIOD: *ODES* 1–3, *EPISTLES* 1

1. *Odes* 1–3

A. Introduction

The first three books of *Odes* have been the most popular of Horace's works in modern scholarship, as they have consistently been his most popular poems since the Renaissance. This popularity has meant that they have played a key role as objects of modern Latin scholarship's particular concerns and developments – for example intertextuality, genre, metapoetry, the poetic book, narratology, and political colouring. This chapter will try to highlight the most important and stimulating items of scholarship from a vast range of work.[1]

B. Fundamentals

In the last half-century the study of the first three books of *Odes* has been much advanced by the emergence of a series of important modern commentaries. Fraenkel's *Horace* (1957) appeared at much the same time as the last edition of the classic German Kiessling–Heinze commentary (1960), which had held the field for mid-scale scholarly exegesis since 1884. Both works in some sense presented the culmination of the humane and learned German scholarship which had dominated Europe since the middle of the nineteenth century, and are still necessary reading for today's Horatian scholars. The new era of modern commentary opened with the publication of Nisbet and Hubbard's commentary on the first book of *Odes* (1970). Its unparalleled depth of material on Roman cultural background, Greek and Latin literary models, and (sometimes) elements of later reception makes it still a treasure trove for scholars and interpreters; even if some of its literary judgements have not stood the test of time, it was an important step to make them and to question from time to time the perfection of a canonical writer. Their second volume, on Book 2,

---

[1] For the period 1945–75 Babcock 1981 is a helpful guide to criticism of the *Odes*.

appeared in 1978; for the third volume, on Book 3 (2004), Niall Rudd replaced Margaret Hubbard as Robin Nisbet's collaborator, yielding a more compact texture. The current generation should be most grateful for this wave of work, which transforms the environment of a half-century ago.

These commentaries will not be quickly replaced, but their very depth and inclusivity has meant that there has been a need for shorter works for more practical use. Perhaps most significant here is Syndikus' running commentary on all the *Odes* (1972–3, third edition 2001), which (as already noted in Chapter I) consists of essays covering the key points in each poem, providing a clear and balanced interpretation of the crucial details and allusions. Important too are the personal and illuminating commentaries on the first three books of the *Odes* by David West (1995, 1998, 2002), which carry forward the lively and penetrating approach to the poet seen in his *Reading Horace* (West 1967): these present the text with parallel translation and running-commentary essays which focus on the key points of interpretation, always with stimulating ideas. The format of these volumes was owed to the similar commentary on Book 3 by Gordon Williams (1969), which was pioneering in this direction and is still worth consultation. Another work much used by students is the commentary on all the *Odes* by Kenneth Quinn (1980), embodying the principles of practical literary criticism for which he was an important standard-bearer in the 1960s and 1970s (best seen in his *Latin Explorations* [1963] which contains some interesting pieces on Horace); it provides some interesting reactions to the commentaries of Nisbet and Hubbard. Useful too are the Italian commentaries on individual odes by Ghiselli (1974, second edition 1983, on 1.1) and Mondin (1997, on 1.4), and on selected odes from the first two books by Baldo (2009).

C. Topics

On poetic technique, Collinge 1961 is an interesting formal analysis of the design of the *Odes*, stressing word order and sequence of thought as the two central and complementary techniques, with a considerable interest in imagery. His emphasis on patterning derives at least partly from linguistic theory, and can sometimes seem overdone; but it does rightly point to the importance of internal dynamics in the *Odes* and the complex formal principles of their construction. Commager's influential book (1962), perhaps the first major work on Horace fully to embody the impact of the New Criticism with its focus on the poetic artefact, presents the significance of the poems as lying primarily in their imagery and emotional colouring. Like Collinge, Commager is interested in structural principles on both small and large scale, especially elements of contrast and tension in both word and thought; he also argues for the presence of parody and allegory, and provides salutary arguments against the biographical approach which had been so powerful up to and including Fraenkel's work. Both these volumes, along with West 1967 and 1973, are also antidotes to the austere judgement of Nisbet and Hubbard that Horace's metaphors are 'sparse and trite',[2] though their more literary articles allow more than this.[3] Another notable contribution in this general domain is the collection of articles by Pöschl (1970), providing a useful series of analyses of particular odes, stressing their symbolic and linguistic richness, and giving good models of dense and critical reading. Wit and humour have sometimes been underemphasized in the *Odes*: West 1967 and especially Connor 1987 provide good evidence for the contrary view.

Another area where there has been considerable debate is that of the ordering of the poems in the poetic books of the *Odes*. Nisbet and Hubbard had here provided some cautious remarks, pointing to the importance of opening and closing poems and sequences, central positioning, thematic groupings, and metrical arrangements, but adding that it was easy to be fanciful in this area.[4] Metrical sequences at least provide hard data: the fact that the so-called 'parade odes' 1.1–9 deploy nine different Greek lyric metres, using tighter rules than Horace's Greek predecessors,[5] is clearly a statement of technical mastery, just as the use of a wide range of lyric predecessors in the following 1.12–18 shows the poet's command of his inherited thematic material.[6] Dettmer 1983 posited a series of complex structural relationships between poems across *Odes* 1–3, many of which can be questioned, while both Santirocco 1986 and D. Porter 1987 argue that the poet has designed *Odes* 1–3 with the close attention to structure of a modern poet, with each poem having a detailed and particular relationship to

---

[2] Nisbet and Hubbard 1970: xxii.
[3] Nisbet 1962; Hubbard 1973.
[4] Nisbet and Hubbard 1970: xxiii–iv.
[5] For this and other key facts on metre in the *Odes*, see Nisbet and Hubbard 1970: xxxviii–xlvi.
[6] Lowrie 1995.

the poems either side of it. Santirocco's scheme is more flexible than Porter's and perhaps more attractive, but there is always a danger of forced interpretation in the construction of such schemes and especially in claiming them for the poet's own intentions. Minarini 1989 provides an interesting survey of the various further schemes of arrangement.

There has also been much discussion of intra-poem structure, moving on from the work of Collinge. Quinn's 1980 commentary commendably suggests an architectural structure for each ode, and Nisbet and Hubbard themselves had been clear in their introduction that the odes were carefully planned with impressive symmetry and unity,[7] though this was not generally pursued in their detailed commentary. Syndikus 1995 looked at different modes of movement within Horace's odes, from personal endings through inversions, through reflections moving away from concrete situations, to ring composition; the last idea was also taken up by Tarrant 1995, who explored Horace's tendency to return to an idea in the final section of a poem.

The 1990s saw an explosion of interest in poetic closure in ancient literature.[8] In Horatian studies this had partly been anticipated in the work of Schrijvers (1973) on how to end an ode and in Esser's monograph (1976) on the ends of all the odes, but Horace was a key point of reference in the more subtly theorized work on poetic closure of Don Fowler.[9] Meanwhile, the opening poems of all Horace's books are touched on by Gold (1992) in the standard volume on classical poetic openings, and the middle points of Horatian poems also receive treatment in Harrison 2004, in the standard collection on poetic middles in antiquity, following the pioneering work of Moritz (1968).

A major work of Horatian criticism is Davis 1991, which put the idea of metapoetry (poetry symbolically talking about poetry) firmly on the map of scholarship on the *Odes*. Davis, a pupil of E. L. Bundy who had famously applied structured rhetorical criticism to the lyrics of Pindar, argues that 'the composer of the *Odes* is primarily engaged in conveying ideas and philosophical insights in a manner that is rhetorically persuasive'.[10] Perhaps surprisingly, he avoids reference to the individuals who are in fact addressed and in theory urged to action in the poems, and I would still agree with Nisbet and Hubbard, whose interpretations of

---

[7] Nisbet and Hubbard 1970: xxiii.
[8] See especially Dunn et al. 1997.
[9] Collected in Fowler 2000.
[10] Davis 1991: 2.

odes try to assign importance to the addressee where possible. Davis looks at many of Horace's odes in a metaphorical way as defining their own form of lyric: talk of the symposium is also talk of symposiastic poetry and of the poet's values and approach to life.[11] Particularly attractive and convincing here is the interpretation of *Odes* 1.38, which for Nisbet and Hubbard is a rather unemphatic end to the first book; in Davis' hands the modest garland, symposium, and lifestyle become a symbol for the unambitious poetry of Horace, the restrained discourse of symposiastic lyric. Another important element stressed by Davis is what he calls 'intergeneric badinage' and 'generic disavowal' – witty contact between Horatian lyric and other genres, which are confronted and then rejected (epic, elegy, tragedy). Another advocate of metapoetry is Krasser (1995), who argues that the divine scenes narrated in the *Odes* often function as a symbol of the poet's own concerns, which can be both literary and political (and indeed both simultaneously), and that the odes related to Bacchus in particular (2.19 and 3.25) serve to express the poet's elevated status and interests. Edmunds 1992 has provided a paradigmatic reading of *Odes* 1.9 from the perspective of reception theory.

Scholars had long been aware of what Kroll 1924 had called *Kreuzung der Gattungen*, 'the interbreeding of genres', the ways in which Horace's odes and other Augustan poems combine and exploit elements of different literary kinds,[12] but the work of Nisbet and Hubbard in carefully identifying in their introduction the various literary genres at play in the *Odes* constituted a stimulus to further work.[13] Conte 1980 and 1986 had shown how Virgil in particular had exploited this element, and its impact on the *Odes* was shown by a number of scholars including Lowrie 1997, who in an important volume showed how many of Horace's more extensive lyric pieces conducted a complex dialogue with narrative forms such as epic and epyllion. Harrison 2007b followed this by arguing that these contacts with other genres resulted in 'generic enrichment', the lyric texture of the odes being permanently expanded through incorporation of non-lyric 'guest' elements. Some of this thinking was certainly influenced by the approach to poetic genre in Cairns 1972, which, though it focused on 'genres of content' derived from rhetorical treatises, pursued the

---

[11] Here his argument has been extended by Mindt 2007.
[12] Cf. Barchiesi 2001a.
[13] Nisbet and Hubbard 1970: xiii–xvii.

same kind of intergeneric analysis of Horatian odes among its many examples.

The relationship of Horace to Greek lyric has always been a key element in Horatian scholarship. Our knowledge and understanding of Greek lyric has increased considerably in recent decades, and with it a greater sense of Horace's interaction with its texts. Useful analyses are found in the handbooks to Horace: Hutchinson 2007 gives a good survey for the Cambridge *Companion*, but the articles in the Blackwell *Companion* are especially useful: Davis (2010b) himself argues with excellent illustrations that the non-iambic poetry of Archilochus is much more important for the odes than previously thought; Strauss Clay 2010 on Lesbian lyric models rightly suggests that Horace aimed to include all Greek lyric in his collection, and stresses the value of Alcaeus for the allegorical interpretation of 1.14 (well known) and the importance of Sappho for the erotics of 4.1 (less well known and very interesting); Race 2010 on Pindar contains excellent detailed analyses of a number of Pindarically coloured odes, stressing the encomiastic elements common to the two poets and containing a number of excellent links.

Important from the 1990s are Feeney 1993, which shows convincingly how Horace fulfils the ambition of *Odes* 1.1 in incorporating himself into the Greek lyric canon and uses all its variety in his own varied output, and Lowrie 1995, which persuasively argues how a sequence of poems in Book 1 symbolically uses material from a range of Greek poets to show the variety of their Horatian remodelling. Barchiesi 2000 has shown that the ordering of Greek lyric collections had important consequences for their reception by Horace, while Woodman 2002 has suggested that Sappho deserves more prominence as a model for Horace than she has traditionally been given and that Catullus' Sapphic imitations and their ambivalent approach to gender were a crucial element here. The discovery of new material by Simonides has similarly led to the reassessment of his impact on Horace's odes,[14] while a significant conference volume presents some important perspectives on a range of issues in the area of Horace and Greek lyric poetry.[15] There has also been some discussion of the so-called 'motto' technique, by which the opening of a Greek poem is alluded to at the opening of a Horatian poem;[16] older views used

[14] Barchiesi 1996, 2001c; Harrison 2001a.
[15] Paschalis 2002.
[16] See especially Cavarzere 1996. For the term, see Fraenkel 1957: 159 n. 2.

to suggest that the Latin poem then tended to go its own way, but we always need to remember that often the first line is all that survives for the Greek poem, and that its lost parts may also be echoed: *Odes* 1.37 is a case in point, where further elements such as the rare Homericizing simile of lines 17–20, as well as the famous opening (cf. Alcaeus *PMG* 332), may come from the Alcaean model.

The influence of the surviving Roman poets of the previous generation on the *Odes* has also been a continuing object of investigation: Putnam 2006 has provided a comprehensive treatment of Catullan intertexts in Horace, showing for example how the two Sapphic poems in Catullus are both echoed in *Odes* 1.22 (1.22.23 = Catullus 51.5; 1.22.5–8 ~ Catullus 11.2–9), while links in the more philosophical *Odes* 2 with Lucretius and his recent promotion of Epicurean ethical values in poetry have also been recently emphasized (Harrison 2013b). We can only guess at the allusions to lost poetry such as those apparently present in 2.9 to the elegist Valgius.[17]

The politics of the *Odes* has been another central topic of discussion,[18] especially the complex Roman Odes (3.1–6), which have been intriguingly argued to be one single poem.[19] Witke 1983 provides a running commentary on all six odes, which provides interesting interpretations and a full bibliography, while Lowrie 1997 gives perhaps the most stimulating recent account, emphasizing how the poet preserves his independence in the cycle through an oblique and lyric approach to Augustan encomium. Fraenkel's narrative of Horace's gradual transformation across the *Odes* into an encomiastic laureate figure has naturally been complicated in the post-1960s period, with the emergence of quite different approaches to the relationship between poetry and power. One influential approach has been that of La Penna (1963), who prefers the aesthetic to the political in his analysis of the *Odes*; the real Horace is the thoughtful and urbane individual of the private odes, not the public *uates* of the political poetry, where La Penna finds a lack of authenticity of sentiment. An interesting contrast with La Penna is Doblhofer (1966, 1981), who followed Pöschl 1956 in stressing the importance of the literary tradition of panegyric in Horace's political odes, but combined this with Fraenkel's belief that Horace was fully sincere in his praises of the great man Augustus.

---

[17] See, for example, Holzberg 2008.
[18] For a useful survey of views to 1992, see Cremona 1993.
[19] Griffiths 2002.

By contrast, more recent scholarship has stressed the gaps and slippages in the *Odes'* relationship with the Augustan regime. Lyne 1995 argues that Horace in the political odes of Book 1–3 mixes deference to the great with assertions of his own social and political status, and sometimes shows a mildly subversive independence, while Lowrie 1997 has, in her own words, explored 'how Horace's decisions about his genre and self-imposed formal constraints give him an excuse for not delving into the central narrative of the age: civil war and Augustus' accession to power'.[20] Don Fowler (1995) has even argued that effective Augustan panegyric is in fact impossible for Horace given his self-consciously modest and individualist ethical and critical framework: 'the inheritance of Epicurean and Stoic moral philosophy on which Horace draws throughout his work ... particularly when conjoined with Callimachean poetics to produce a Callimachean ethics, makes it impossible to produce successful panegyric'.[21] Seager 1993, on the other hand, argued that Horace became disillusioned with Augustan foreign policy owing to his personal commitment to imperial expansion. The issue still continues to divide scholars, much as in the study of Virgil.

Closely linked with politics is the issue of patronage. Syme 1939 had influentially suggested that the poets wrote what was convenient to their political masters in this period; Fraenkel 1957 (ignoring Syme) presents a narrative of growing affection and alignment between poet and *princeps*, while White (1993, 2007) shows how the relationship between poet and patron was simply one variety of the complex framework of *amicitia* within Rome's privileged classes, in which the poets firmly stood. More recently, frameworks from anthropology have been creatively applied to this discussion: Bowditch (2001, 2010) persuasively suggests that Horace artfully presents his patronage relationship with Maecenas and Augustus as combining proper gratitude with the putative reciprocity of a gift economy, and as allowing for the negotiation of some independence alongside moments of anxiety. The relationship between Horace and Maecenas has naturally stood at the centre of this debate, with its characteristics both of friendship between like-minded equals and of power and obligation: Horace's odes to Maecenas have been well discussed by Santirocco and Lyne, among others.[22]

---

[20] Lowrie 2009a: 5.
[21] Fowler 1995: 267.
[22] Santirocco 1986: 153–66 (earlier version reprinted in Lowrie 2009a); Lyne 1995: 102–38.

A key feature of the *Odes* is that they normally have an addressee. One of the signal services of the Nisbet–Hubbard and Nisbet–Rudd commentaries is that they take the status of the addressee seriously, and use the resources of the prosopographical approach to Roman history to track down detail on identifiable addressees, not always to universal assent. They crucially show that the addressee is not (as some have thought) window-dressing for universal lyric thoughts left over from an archaic context of performance, but a real determinant for the poem's content; West 1973 importantly pushes in the same direction. As Citroni argues in the most important modern account of the *Odes*' use of the addressee, this particularity need not exclude ethical generalizing, and indeed makes it more effective and accessible to the reader by pinning a moral precept to the vivid context of an individual.[23] It is still important to remember that, 'perhaps oftener than we know, Horace's choice of imagery and vocabulary is determined by the personality and interests of a poem's recipient',[24] especially as many modern treatments of the *Odes* tend to stress their poetic autonomy as lyric poems rather than their situatedness as artefacts produced in a certain cultural environment. This emphasis on the reader – both the original implied reader and his/her successors – follows the turn to the reconstructible reader rather than the less reconstructible author in the interpretation of literature generally. This is a less theorized version of reader-response theory, with which classical literary studies meshes nicely.[25]

Another major issue is that of performance. Until recently, most followed the view of Heinze 1923 that the references to lyres and singing in the *Odes* were simply fictional allusions to the tradition of archaic Greek lyric performance rather than indications of musical performance of the *Odes*.[26] More recently, with increased interest in the element of performance and song in Greek and Roman literature,[27] the issue of actual performance of the *Odes* has again been raised.[28] Perhaps the most plausible approach is that of Lowrie 2009b, which suggests that too much is made of the contrast between the function of an original

---

[23] Citroni 1995: 271–376 (English version in Lowrie 2009a).

[24] Hubbard 1973: 18.

[25] See e.g. Harrison 2001c: 11. For interesting work on the poet's construction and manipulation of the reader in the *Odes*, see e.g. Sutherland 2002.

[26] See, for example, Rossi 1998. English translations of both Heinze and Rossi in Lowrie 2009a.

[27] For the latter, see e.g. Habinek 2005.

[28] E.g. Murray 1985; Lefèvre 1993; Lyons 2007.

performance in a real historical context and that of a purely textual reading of a poem. In some poems at least, as she sees it, the idea of repeated performance is invoked as a symbol of repeated reading and social continuity, just like repeated textual copying on paper.

The erotic odes and their approach to gender have been more closely scrutinized in an age when feminist scholarship has come to bear on Latin literature.[29] Lyne 1980 showed that in general Horace's erotic odes regard love as a playful activity for the youthful and leisured, and as a temporary and varied pastime, rather than as the obsession with a single lover seen in Roman elegy, though he did not allow for odes such as 3.9, which seem to cede something (however ironically) to the idea of lifelong commitment. An independent and stimulating, if sometimes eccentric, treatment of the love odes is offered by Nadeau 2008; Minadeo 1982 takes a more Freudian approach in analysing their sexual symbolism, opening up an important area, if occasionally too enthusiastically.

It is hard to deny that Horace 'is a poet more for men than for women':[30] even considering the unliberated standards of the period, Horace gives less dignity and air-time to the female characters of the *Odes* than do the love elegists, though here he is perhaps following the literary traditions of archaic Greek lyric and Hellenistic epigram: too often they are types (Pyrrha [1.5] as femme fatale, Chloe [1.23] as timid adolescent, Lydia [1.25] as too old for the game of love). The degree of fictionality with which erotic objects are presented, a problem in Roman poetry since Catullus, has a particular prominence in Horace's *Odes*, where the love objects are many and their names are often punning or symbolic: Pyrrha's name reflects her attractive hair colour and 'fiery' (Greek *pyrrhos*) temperament, Chloe's her youth (Greek *chloe*, 'green shoot'), Lydia's both her ethnic/servile origins and her role as 'play-girl' (*ludere*). There is clearly a balance here between literary function and realism.[31] A more nuanced and sophisticated approach is offered by Ancona 1994, which shows how the themes of time and desire identified by Lyne give us a world where, in the end, the male lover cannot control things and love remains an elusive target; more recently, in Ancona 2010, she has given us a useful sketch of Horace's female characters from this perspective.

---

[29] See, for example, Richlin 1991.
[30] Oliensis 2007: 221.
[31] For the latter, see Griffin 1985.

The *Odes'* depiction of the symposium has been a renewed topic of interest following recent research into symposiastic culture generally.[32] In the field of Horatian studies this has given further support to the fresh interest in whether or not the odes were performed in such contexts,[33] as well as in whether the kinds of symposium that the *Odes* depict were realistic for Augustan Rome.[34] Most successful perhaps here are approaches which take a more symbolic view: the symposium can express not just moderate Epicurean hedonism but also a moderate style of poetry suitable for lyric, set in the middle ground between the heights of epic and tragedy and the lower forms of elegy and comedy.[35] The details of the symposium can thus take on a metapoetical tinge, especially in *Odes* 1.38, where the presentation of a moderate symposium in the final brief poem of a long book surely reflects the author's Callimachean poetics of brevity.[36] Wine itself can be symbolic of poetry through their shared patron Bacchus,[37] who can push lyric to heights of inspiration;[38] particular vintages can also recall small facts about the addressee.[39]

The philosophical perspective of the *Odes* has often been a subject of discussion. We are still without a major modern monograph on philosophy in Horace, partly because it is such a ubiquitous presence in all his work. Some see Horace as strongly concerned with philosophical didacticism, especially in ethics, while others view philosophy as simply part of the intellectual material of the time: Moles 2007 presents the best brief survey of the issue and discussion of other work, and full references are provided by Mariotti.[40] The *Odes* in general present something of an eclectic world: the Epicurean elements of the erotic and symposiastic odes, with their emphasis on moderate pleasure, the undesirability of anxiety, and the brevity of life, clearly point towards an Epicurean perspective; in contrast, the more elevated world of the Roman Odes (3.1–6) takes on the Stoic ideas of virtue, duty, activism, and patriotism which spoke naturally to Roman culture, and holds up enduring national heroes such as Regulus as models for imitation. It

---

[32] E.g. Murray 1990.
[33] Murray 1985.
[34] Griffin 1985.
[35] Mette 1961.
[36] See especially Davis 1991: 118–26.
[37] Commager 1957, reprinted in Lowrie 2009a.
[38] Davis 2007.
[39] Cf. Nisbet 1959.
[40] Mariotti 1996–8: ii.78–98.

is also clear that some odes (such as those to Maecenas) reflect the likely philosophical views of their addressee.

2. *Epistles* 1

A. Introduction

In the last generation, the first book of *Epistles* has moved from relative neglect to the centre stage in Horatian scholarship. In the 1980s and early 1990s, it could be referred to as having 'second-class status amongst Horace's poetry' and as Horace's 'least (in this era anyway) talked about book'.[41] This was at least partly a function of its only marginal appearance (mentioned only in part, and without commentary) alongside a magisterially full analysis of *Epistles* 2 and the *Ars poetica* in Brink's three great volumes on *Horace on Poetry* (see Chapter V, section 4, below). Before the mid-1980s, apart from Fraenkel's 1957 account, the chief tools for investigation were McGann 1969, which focused on Horace's philosophical sources, and the work of Dilke – his brief commentary (1954), useful interpretative essay (1973), and survey of scholarship for 1959–79 (1981). The chief issues were the seriousness of Horace's ethical stance in this poetry book[42] and the relationship of its poems to real letters.[43] As we shall see, these issues rumble on, but much more sophisticated literary criticism has now been directed at the *Epistles*, resulting in a much more nuanced view of this poetry collection.

B. Fundamentals

As with the *Odes*, the study of the first book of *Epistles* has been much eased by the appearance of a modern English commentary, that of Mayer (1994), which is especially helpful on the work's Latinity and linguistic level; also useful is the extensive Italian running commentary by Fedeli (1997), and the fine book-length commentaries on individual poems by Horsfall (1993) and Citti (1994). We also now have a reliable general guide, Kilpatrick 1986, which provides a sympathetic and

---

[41] Kilpatrick 1986: ix; W. Johnson 1993: ix.
[42] See e.g. Macleod 1979.
[43] E.g. Williams 1968: 1–30; Allen et al. 1972.

approachable reading of all the poems of the book, as well as being well aware of previous scholarship; this is now the first point of call for an extended treatment. For shorter accounts there are useful expert pieces in all three Horace *Companions*: Ferri 2007, Cucchiarelli 2010, W. Johnson 2010, and Fantham 2013a. W. Johnson 1993 provides a dense and wide-ranging personal reading of *Epistles* 1 as a search for different kinds of freedom, whether social, philosophical, or literary.

C. Topics

As noted above, the relationship of *Epistles* 1 to real letters has been a matter of scholarly discussion. Most would now agree that what we have here are highly artistic poems which make literary capital out of exploiting their resemblance to actual letters, just like Ovid's later *Heroides* and *Tristia*. Many of the topics of the letters match those of a real correspondence (1.2, 1.4, 1.10: letter to a friend from vacation or the country; 1.3, 1.8, 1.11, 1.15: letter to a friend on campaign or travels abroad; 1.5: letter of invitation; 1.6, 1.17, 1.18: letter of advice; 1.7: letter of excuse; 1.9, 1.12: letter of recommendation; 1.13: covering letter for gift of books; 1.14: letter to a member of staff), but the programmatic opening referring to Horace's past writing career (1.1), the reply to critics of his previous poetry (1.19), and the witty address to the book as a slave going abroad (1.20), alluding to the final poems of *Odes* 2.20 and 3.30,[44] all show that this is a hexameter *sermo* poetry book in the same general tradition as the *Satires*. Recent work on epistolary frameworks in the English novel[45] has been applied with fruitful results to *Epistles* 1 by De Pretis (2002), who nicely shows how these poems interact with many features of ancient letter-writing,[46] to some extent deconstructing the dichotomy between 'real' and 'literary' letters. It is even possible to suggest that Horace's book obeys some of the precepts of ancient epistolographical theory.[47]

Literary models for letters existed in philosophical and satiric predecessors: Plato, Aristotle, and Epicurus all had epistles attached to their names (some extant, in prose and lengthy), while some of Lucilius' satires were clearly verse letters of a kind, which provided a model

---

[44] See Harrison 1988.
[45] Altman 1982.
[46] Itself now a highly fashionable area of research: see Morello and Morrison 2007.
[47] Harrison 1995c.

for epistolary verse in hexameter *sermo* (e.g. fr. 186–9 W.), and Sp.
Mummius, brother and legate to L. Mummius, the conqueror of
Corinth in 146 BCE, had sent back humorous verse letters to his friends
at Rome (Cicero *Att.* 13.6.4). Horace may already have known Cicero's
Ad familiares, an example of a carefully arranged corpus of letters
addressed to friends by a major literary figure. And, of course, *Odes*
1–3 already provided a precedent for a poetry book in which individual
items were addressed to and tailored for different friends, a number of
whom recur in *Epistles* 1; apart from Maecenas in 1.1, 1.7, and 1.19, we
have Albius (Tibullus) in 1.5 (cf. *Odes* 1.33), Septimius in 1.9 (cf. *Odes*
2.6), Fuscus in 1.10 (cf. *Odes* 1.22), Iccius in 1.12 (cf. *Odes* 1.29), and
Quinctius in 1.16 (cf. *Odes* 2.11). As in the links with the *Satires*, there
are considerable continuities between the *Epistles* and the *Odes*.

The philosophical content of the book has been a major issue: how
seriously are we to take the apparent 'conversion' of the poet raised
in *Epistles* 1.1.10–12, and his apparently programmatic statement of
tentative eclecticism in the same poem, claiming to veer between the
extremes of austere Stoicism and soft Aristippean hedonism (1.1.16–
18)? Macleod 1979, undoubtedly influenced by the rather positivistic
analysis of conversion narratives in later antiquity by Nock 1933,
argued for a genuine turn to ethics in Horace's middle age, and for a
genuine commitment both to the betterment of his addressees and to
self-improvement. Most recent scholarship, however, has taken the programme for a poetic one rather than a personal one, pointing out that
the crucial line *condo et compono quae mox depromere possim* (1.1.12) can
mean either 'I put in store and lay aside things to bring out in due
course' (i.e. gather wisdom for future use) or 'I compose and put
together things to bring out in due course' (i.e. write poetry), and
that Horace's philosophical interests in the *Epistles*, though differently
framed in didactic terms, are consistent with those in the *Odes* and
Satires. Mayer 1986 suggests a broad Socratic approach to the subject,
and the same scholar has highlighted the collection's interest in such
general social virtues as tact (Mayer 1985).

Nevertheless, this has not stopped scholars from proposing particular
philosophical affiliations for the first book of *Epistles*, following the lead
of McGann 1969's suggestions of links with Panaetian Stoicism.[48]
Traina 1991 has suggested that Horace's own doctrinal profession of

---

[48] Stoicism was also supported by Maurach 1968.

moving between Stoicism and Aristippean hedonism is to be taken seriously (some might say that they are simply typical polar opposites stated rhetorically). Meanwhile, Moles 2002 and 2007 demonstrate well
that allusion to a wide range of philosophical doctrines is crucial to
Horace's book, that the poet's eclecticism constitutes a positive freedom rather than a weak vacillation, and that philosophical doctrines
on such matters as the quiet life have a real impact on his existence.
Ferri 1993, a suggestive and sensitive reading of the book, suggests
that Horace is a moderate Epicurean, shying away from the high didacticism of Lucretius and practising a more personal and tentative form of
his philosophy in a rustic retreat, the *angulus* or quiet corner; Armstrong
2004 stresses the links with the Epicurean poet and philosopher
Philodemus. Most recently, Morrison 2007 has suggested that there
is closer engagement with Lucretius in *Epistles* 1, the book mirroring
the 'plot' of the didactic poem, with the poet as progressing pupil; it
is certainly clear that the poet presents himself not as an established
sage but as a developing fellow-seeker for truth in company with the
reader.[49]

---

[49] Cf. e.g. Harrison 1995c.

V LATE PERIOD: *CARMEN SAECULARE, ODES 4, EPISTLES 2, ARS POETICA*

1. Introduction

Carl Becker's 1963 book defined all these works plus the first book of *Epistles* as constituting Horace's late work, partly because (in the biographizing fashion of the time) he saw *Epistles* 1 as the decisive beginning of a final and mature period for the poet, focused on philosophical and ethical retirement and distanced contemplation of poetry and the world. In this volume I have chosen to assign the first book of *Epistles* not to the later period but to the middle period with the *Odes* (see Chapter IV), partly because I hold that it is not so different from the *Odes* in its concerns and techniques, even if it constitutes a move from lyric back to the hexameter *sermo* which Horace had last used ten years before, and partly because I take the philosophical programme of *Epistles* 1 as a statement about the book's particular content rather than about the poet's life in general.

Becker dated *Epistles* 2.2 to 19 BCE and the *Ars poetica* to 18 BCE. The latter at least is not much favoured by modern scholarship: most are now moving to the idea that the *Ars* is a final massive statement on poetry capping the views of *Epistles* 2, perhaps even originally intended as part of that book – see Chapter II above. However, it seems clear in general terms that these poems of Horace's last decade are written from the perspective of a senior poet, perhaps the last of the great Augustan generation, following Virgil's death *c.*19 BCE and the likely silence of Propertius after his final book of elegies *c.*16 BCE. In this period national/political interests and (especially) literary didacticism predominate over more 'frivolous' themes, which are effectively rounded off in the fourth book of *Odes*.

2. *Carmen saeculare*

After languishing for some years in the shadows, the *Carmen saeculare* has in the last generation emerged into the full light of scholarly scrutiny.[1] Critics have begun to realize that this seventy-six-line poem, though composed in the Sapphic stanza, the second most popular metre in the *Odes*, is no mere appendage but fundamentally distinctive within Horatian lyric.[2] It was written (as an inscription confirms[3]) in the first-person plural for performance by a choir of twenty-seven boys and twenty-seven girls in the ritual context of the *ludi saeculares* at Rome on 3 June 17 BCE.[4] This presents a major contrast with the usual single voice of the rest of Horatian lyric (see Chapter IV). Modern scholarship has been much concerned with working out how the text of the poem relates to its religious context,[5] but has also provided in-depth readings of the poem as a literary artefact,[6] and explorations of its affinities within performed Greek lyric genres such as the paean.[7] The fact that this is the one poem of the Augustan period for which we have firm external evidence for a performance context has naturally moved it to the centre of the recent debate about performance elements in Roman poetry.[8] In terms of style and structure, its somewhat prosaic language can be linked to its ritual context, with its need to point to particular divinities and features of their cults, while its triadic structure (six groups of three stanzas each plus a final single epode) plainly looks back to Greek choral lyric.

3. *Odes* 4

The claim of the 'Suetonian' biography of Horace (see Chapter II) that the fourth book of *Odes* grew from Augustus' commissioning of *Odes* 4.4 and 4.14 for the two princes Tiberius and Drusus, which stimulated a return to lyric odes after a long interval, looks likely to be a conjecture from the prominent presence of these poems in the book. It seems more probable that Horace's return to a different type of lyric through the commission of the *Carmen saeculare* of 17 BCE led to more lyric poems in the manner of *Odes* 1–3, and, as critics point out, memories

---

[1] Though Fraenkel 1957: 364–82 devoted a substantial analysis to the poem.
[2] See Barchiesi 2002.
[3] *CIL* 6.32323, now conveniently accessible in Thomas 2011: 173–6.
[4] For a full treatment of the festival context, see Schnegg-Köhler 2002; for a useful summary Thomas 2011: 53–7.
[5] Feeney 1998: 32–8.
[6] Putnam 2000; Günther 2013b.
[7] Barchiesi 2002.
[8] Habinek 2005: 150–7; Lowrie 2009b: 123–41.

of the *Carmen saeculare* and its dramatic publicity for the poet are a feature of *Odes* 4 (4.3, 4.6). Though political poems predominate in this
book, there are also some poems in the manner of Horace's earlier collection, especially in its later part (4.1, 4.10, 4.11–13). In terms of dating, although some had viewed *Odes* 4 as Horace's latest work,[9] most
would now see the book as written in the period 17–13 BCE and emerging in 13 as Augustus returned from Spain and Gaul (prefigured in
4.2 and 4.5).[10] The publication of a literary work as an anticipatory
celebration of an Augustan return would be paralleled by the probably
appearance of Virgil's *Georgics* in the summer of 29 BCE, in time for the
triple triumph of August of that year.[11]

The fourth book, though given detailed treatment by Fraenkel as the
climax of Horace's career,[12] was not especially popular in the 1960s and
1970s, perhaps because of the predominant political and encomiastic
material, which did not fit the times especially well.[13] Once again,
Michael Putnam deserves some credit for rescuing a Horatian book:
his running commentary (Putnam 1986) was an important stimulus
to further work, and is still the most extensive literary treatment, clearly
showing that the poetic texture of the fourth book matches those of the
earlier ones in complexity and interest. The same is true of the *de facto*
running commentary of T. Johnson 2004, which neatly argues that
Book 4 effectively combines symposiastic and encomiastic elements
in drawing the audience from private to public celebration, while main-
taining a Callimachean witty independence and ambiguity.

The lack of a focused modern conventional commentary outside
those on the whole of the *Odes* by Quinn (1980) and Syndikus
(1972–3, second edition 2001) was also certainly something of a barrier
to the book's study for some years. However, we now have an extensive
Italian commentary by Fedeli and Ciccarelli (2008), which has a good
deal of important material, especially on language, and a major commentary in English by Richard Thomas for Cambridge (2011), which
applies with excellent results its author's characteristic emphasis on
poetic texture and anxieties about encomiastic elements in Augustan
poetry.

[9] E.g. Williams 1972: 44–9.
[10] See the summary discussion in Thomas 2011: 5–7.
[11] See e.g. Harrison 2007b: 154.
[12] Fraenkel 1957: 400–53.
[13] It was certainly the reason why neither Robin Nisbet nor David West wanted to write a commentary on it (personal communication).

The increased encomiastic element in Book 4 is indeed striking. It has been plausibly linked to an increased interest in Pindar, named in 4.2 as inimitable and 4.9 as excellent, and clearly a model for the praise odes of this book. These use Pindaric techniques of victory laudation such as extensive heroic speeches and gnomic utterances, applied here not to Pindaric athletic success but to the parallel triumph of Roman arms.[14] Another significant element is the clear presence among the addressees of the fourth book of a generation of young men rising to prominence under the middle years of the Augustan regime and on the verge of the consulship as Horace writes.[15] *Odes* 4.1 is addressed to Paulus Fabius Maximus, husband (then or later) of Augustus' cousin Marcia and soon to be consul in 11 BCE; 4.2 to Iullus Antonius, son of Antony, brought up in the imperial house and soon to be consul in 10 BCE; 4.4 to the prince Drusus, stepson of Augustus, consul 9 BCE; 4.14 to his brother, the future emperor Tiberius, consul 13 BCE; 4.8 (perhaps) to C. Marcius Censorinus, consul 8 BCE. The *princeps* himself is directly addressed in 4.5 and 4.15, really for the first time by Horace in his *Odes* (1.2 and 1.12 had praised him, the Roman Odes had evoked him at a distance, and 3.14 had welcomed him back in the third person). Maecenas is restricted to one (warm) mention in fifteen odes (4.11.19–20), perhaps indicating continuing friendship but a naturally diminished role as the poet's channel to the *princeps*, who was now personally connected with Horace after the *Carmen saeculare* and more available to him in Rome in the teens BCE.[16]

Alongside this more political element sits erotic and sympotic material recognizably akin to that of the first three books. The book begins (4.1) with a supposed resurgence of erotic feelings in the poet, this time unrequited passion for the boy Ligurinus, also the addressee of an epigram-style poem which warns him against unkindness to lovers, given that he will lose his looks in time (4.10). These poems surely point symbolically to the reprise of erotic lyric rather than to a real obsessive passion, and to the potential inappropriateness of erotic poetry for an ageing poet past fifty (4.1.4–6). The same message emerges from 4.11, inviting Phyllis to a party, with the claim that she

[14] See e.g. Harrison 1990, 1995b.
[15] Syme 1986: 396–402.
[16] Augustus was away from Rome for most of 32–29, 27–24, 22–19, and 16–13: see the convenient chart in Eck 2007: 166–7.

is his last female lover, readily interpreted as a metapoetical statement that the poet is now coming to the end of his lyric output. In 4.13 the poet rejoices that Lyce has become old but also laments his own ageing, while the famous spring ode (4.7) greets the cyclic return of the seasons but also looks forward to the final stage of the human life cycle in death. This material is self-consciously the work of a poet who has passed the youth appropriate to love and is looking to the end of his lyric career: the opening presentation of Venus as goddess of love in 4.1 is balanced and capped by her role as national goddess in 4.15.[17]

An interesting problem is set by 4.12, addressed to a Vergilius and replete with allusions to the poetry of Virgil, but this Virgil is alive and socializing with young men, whereas the great poet has been dead for several years by *Odes* 4. Is this a poem with a past dramatic date, or is this Vergilius not the poet? Various views have been expressed:[18] one possibility not yet adequately discussed is that this could be a living relative of the dead poet (hence the Vergilian allusions, but an addressee still alive after 19 BCE). It would certainly be unparalleled for a Horatian ode to be addressed to a dead person as if he were alive.

4. *Epistles* 2 and *Ars poetica*

Following discussions on dating since Becker 1963, scholarship seems to be moving towards a consensus that both *Epistles* 2.1 and the *Ars poetica* belong to the very last phase of Horace's career, between *Odes* 4 (*c.*13 BCE) and Horace's death in 8 BCE. A more disputed issue has been the dating of *Epistles* 2.2: its sharing of an addressee (Florus) with *Epistles* 1.3 and its apparent reference to the same military service with Tiberius there mentioned (2.2.1~1.3.1–2) have usually led to a dating about the same time as *Epistles* 1 (19 BCE), but this leaves a poetic book with two items, one of which (the second) is some seven years earlier than the other. A recent development has been the argument that the reference to Florus' faithful service points to his being with Tiberius since the previous poem some years before: the poet thus praises his friend's laudable loyalty to his commander over a

---

[17] See Fantham 2013b: 445, in a sympathetic account of the book.
[18] Conveniently gathered by Thomas 2011: 226–7.

considerable time.[19] This leaves us with the possibility that both *Epistles* 2.1 and *Epistles* 2.2 can belong to the same period, *c.*12–8 BCE.

The date of the *Ars poetica* seems to have settled down after a period of some debate.[20] Williams 1972, agreeing roughly with Becker 1963, had argued for an early date of 23–17 BCE, and a date of 23–20 was proposed following stylometric affinity with *Epistles* 1 by Frischer 1991, but most have now accepted Syme's arguments about the identity of the addressees as the sons of Piso the Pontifex, and the consequent need for the poem to be published after Piso's own absence from Rome in 12–10 BCE.[21] Caution pinning down a clear date for the *Ars* is still expressed by Brink,[22] but he too is generally inclined to date it after *Odes* 4.[23] Williams had already suggested that, given its epistolary form and literary concerns, the *Ars poetica* would naturally form a Horatian poetry book of normal length with *Epistles* 2.1 and 2.2 (a feeling shared by Kilpatrick), which he would have dated to *c.*17 BCE.[24] Harrison 2008 has taken these ideas further, arguing that the *Ars poetica* was conceived as the climax of *Epistles* 2, though its apparent early separation from the rest of the book in the transmission and indirect tradition (it is cited as *Ars poetica* as early as Quintilian 8.3.60) might suggest that it was published posthumously and separately. The idea that it might originally have been intended as *Epistles* 2.3 has been regularly considered by scholars,[25] and there seems little doubt in general that the *Ars poetica* is closely bound to *Epistles* 2.1 and 2.2 through its epistolary framework and literary-ethical didacticism.

This unity is underlined in the massive enterprise of Brink's *Horace on Poetry*, which in three volumes over a period of several decades (Brink 1963, 1971, 1982) produced texts, commentaries, and literary considerations of all three poems, *Epistles* 2.1 and 2.2, and the *Ars poetica*. Of these, *Epistles* 2.1, with its address to Augustus, had received a substantial treatment in Fraenkel 1957, but the other two poems were conspicuous by their absence from that book, which left Brink ample room for manoeuvre. In many ways, Brink's work here is parallel to that of Nisbet and Hubbard on the *Odes*, bringing to bear a huge

---

[19] See Harrison 2008 and Chapter II, section 2D, above.
[20] Though note the caution in Reinhardt 2013: 500.
[21] Syme 1986: 379–81. See the clear and helpful summary of the arguments in Rudd 1989: 19–21.
[22] Brink 1982: 554–8.
[23] Brink 1963: 216–17.
[24] Williams 1972: 38–9; Kilpatrick 1990: 55–7.
[25] Brink 1963: 183–4.

panoply of scholarship in the exegesis and interpretation of these difficult poems, and constituting a monumental achievement. Since (unlike
Nisbet and Hubbard) it produces a critical text with apparatus, and
there are more textual difficulties than in the *Odes*, textual discussion
looms much larger, and Brink's discussion of the Horatian transmission has remained authoritative, while his expertise in ancient philosophy and Latin lexicography is clear throughout.[26] Notes in the
commentaries are generous in length and cover a full range of learning
from textual and linguistic to cultural and philosophical, and they are
sometimes hard to navigate; the 962 lines of these three poems receive
(in addition to a substantial volume of general introduction) some 1107
pages of exegesis, more than twice the density of Nisbet and Hubbard
on *Odes* 1 and 2 (775 pages on 1436 lines). This massive commentary,
already a generation old, will not be soon superseded in its philological
and philosophical discussions, though its bibliography (always somewhat backward-looking) is naturally becoming dated, and its literary-
critical interpretations can be debated and questioned.[27]

As with Nisbet and Hubbard, the existence of a vast major scholarly
commentary has stimulated the emergence of smaller-scale works
which incorporate and challenge its findings. The commentary of
Rudd (1989) has done this admirably for all three works, using Brink
circumspectly and independently, and showing itself shrewd and sens-
ible in its interpretations and judgements. Also very useful is Kilpatrick
1990, a fine running commentary on the three poems, which brings out
their shared interests and themes clearly and sympathetically (see also
Kilpatrick 1986), and adds an elegant translation of all three.
Handbook treatments have been similarly effective: Laird 2007 provides a succinct and stimulating account of the *Ars* with an excellent
orientation in modern scholarship, while Günther 2013c gives an
extended literary reading of *Epistles* 2.1 and 2.2, and Reinhardt 2013
argues that the *Ars* is an effective channel for Peripatetic literary criticism and uses techniques for engaging the reader already established
in Latin didactic poetry by Lucretius.

It may be worth pointing out some of the clear thematic similarities
which hold the three poems together, and which can be taken as

---

[26] See Tarrant 1983. Brink's Berlin doctoral thesis in 1933 had been on the pseudo-Aristotelian
Magna moralia, under the direction of Werner Jaeger, and in 1933–8 he had worked on the
Thesaurus Linguae Latinae in Munich – see Jocelyn 2004.

[27] See, for example, the detailed review by Williams (1974).

possible evidence for their planned inclusion in a single book.[28] Both *Epistles* 2.1 and the *Ars* focus on the development of Latin literature from Greek, especially with attention to drama (*Epist.* 2.1.156–67; *Ars* 268–88): the two passages contain the only mentions in all Horace of the names of Thespis (*Epist.* 2.1.163; *Ars* 276) and Aeschylus (*Epist.* 2.1.163; *Ars* 279). Both *Epistles* 2.1 and the *Ars* contain criticism of Plautus, regarded by Horace as crude and undiscriminating (*Epist.* 2.1.170–6; *Ars* 270–4), and of the Alexander-poet Choerilus of Iasos, seen in both poems as an incompetent anti-model for modern epic poets, again mentioned only in these two contexts in all Horace (*Epist.* 2.1.232–3; *Ars* 357–8). The prominent pair of modern epic poets Virgil and Varius is likewise found in these two poems (*Epist.* 2.1.247: *Vergilius Variusque poetae*; cf. *Ars* 55: *Vergilio Varioque*), recalling their pairing in the first book of *Satires* more than twenty years before (*Sat.* 1.5.40–1: *Plotius et Varius Sinuessae Vergiliusque / occurrunt* ['Plotius and Varius and Virgil met us at Sinuessa']; *Sat.* 1.6.54–5: *optimus olim / Vergilius, post hunc Varius, dixere quid essem* ['once excellent Virgil, and after him Varius, said what kind of thing I was']). The double reference is perhaps a career-closing return in a final collection to Horace's first poetry book and a tribute to his now dead poetic friends.

Epistles 2.2 and the *Ars* can be equally well connected. Both begin with famous counterfactual conditions as opening devices – compare *Epistles* 2.2.1–3, 17 ('were someone to try to sell you a slave with a suitable sales patter, he would succeed ...') with *Ars* 1–3, 5 ('were an artist to add a horse's neck to a human head and bird's feathers ... would you not laugh?'). Both poems also contain lists of Horatian genres. At *Epistles* 2.2.59–60 Horace's friends are said to differ in their preferences between *Odes*, *Epodes*, and *sermones*, while *Ars* 79–85 treats key elements of the poet's career with elegant indirection, moving from Archilochus (as the model of the *Epodes*), via a digression about the use of iambics in drama, to a Pindarizing account of lyric which clearly encapsulates the major themes of the *Odes*: hymns, epinicians (no doubt looking to the Pindaric imitations of *Odes* 4), love, and the symposium. Once again, the element of surveying the poet's output, whether explicitly or implicitly, would be appropriate to a unified and self-consciously 'late' book in Horace's poetic career.

All three poems share key thoughts too. Each deals with the theme of the usefulness of the poet to the community: *Epistles* 2.1.124

---

[28] For further discussion, see Harrison 2008.

memorably claims that he can be *utilis urbi* ('of use to the city'), and
Epistles 2.2.121 that the poet will make Latium rich with his language,
while *Ars* 396–401 points to the historic function of poets as law-givers.
Typically, at the end of each poem this dignified idea of the poet's status is conjoined with a more ironic presentation of the same idea.
Epistles 2.1 concludes with the fate of bad poets and their verses
which Horace seeks to avoid (being used to wrap spices: *Epist.*
2.1.267–70); *Epistles* 2.2 with a playful self-address which suggests
that the poet has enjoyed more than enough of the pleasures of life
(*Epist.* 2.2.213–6); and the *Ars* with the celebrated picture of the mad
poet who will not leave his listener alone (*Ars* 453–76).

The poet's direct engagement with the *princeps* in *Epistles* 2.1, the
epistle to Augustus, has attracted particular scholarly attention in recent
years, especially in terms of its political subtexts. Oliensis 1998 has
shown that the poem tackles issues of the poet's status and 'face', pointing to the dangers of literature as gift exchange and noting that Horace
leaves himself out of the list of poets personally patronized by
Augustus.[29] Feeney 2002 argues that the literary-critical content of
the poem necessarily involves political ideology in matters of freedom
of speech, authority, and canon-formation, and that there is a clear ana-
logy between the ageing *princeps*, ruling alone after the death of
Agrippa, and the ageing poet, left alone at the summit of Roman literature after the death of Virgil and others. Lowrie 2009b examines the
issue of the social function of Horatian poetry through the epistle's
stress on the apparent loss of the Greek immediacy of performance in
the written literary culture of Rome, arguing that Horace is conscious
of the inevitable politicizing of performance culture and its conflict
with the tendency of lyric to identify an individual, non-conformist
voice.[30] The same issues have been detected in *Epistles* 2.2:
Freudenburg 2002 locates the poem in an atmosphere of anxiety
about Rome's renewal at the time of the *ludi saeculares* of 17 BCE, detect-
ing consequent political and cultural tensions, and suggesting that
Florus' own interests and legalistic mind-set can be detected in the
epistle addressed to him, while Oliensis 1998 argues that Horace uses
compliments to the younger Florus for his own self-representation
and 'face'.[31]

---

[29] Oliensis 1998: 191–7.
[30] Lowrie 2009b: 235–50.
[31] Oliensis 1998: 7–11.

The *Ars poetica* has been much analysed since Brink's magisterial edition, which not only placed the philological interpretation of the poem on a new level but also opened up a number of avenues of literary treatment. Russell 1973 is a sympathetic reading of the poem as both a work of literature and a work of poetics, with some indications of its major influence on post-Renaissance Western culture; Laird 2007 and Reinhardt 2013, noted above, are sure guides to recent scholarly discussion. One key issue has been the poem's structure: most analysts agree that lines 1–294 treat poetry and the poem while lines 295–476 treat the poet, but further divisions are controversial, as can be seen from comparing the detailed structural schemes in, for example, Brink 1963, Williams 1974, Rudd 1989, and Kilpatrick 1990. Interest has also focused on the presentation of the speaker, following the application of *persona*-theory to Horace's earlier *sermones* (see above, Chapter II): most have seen at least some autobiographical colour in the figure of the poet who has given up non-*sermo* poetry and turned to literary didactic about poets and poetry (*Ars* 306: *nil scribens ipse docebo* ['though writing nothing myself, I will give instruction']), but no self-representation by Horace is straightforward, even if few have followed Frischer's intriguing argument that the *Ars* presents a 'mock-didactic parody of a pedantic speaker not to be confused with Horace himself or his usual poetic persona'.[32] Oliensis 1998 neatly argues that Horace reinforces and advertises his laureate status in the *Ars* by providing instruction for the young which is as much social and cultural as literary and poetic: 'Horace is teaching the Piso brothers how to fashion themselves as well as their poems'.[33]

The third-century-CE commentator Porphyrio (on *Ars* 1) famously reported that Horace drew the critical precepts of the *Ars* from the Hellenistic Peripatetic critic Neoptolemus of Paros (third century BCE), but, apart from a few polemical mentions of Neoptolemus in the literary criticism of Horace's older contemporary the Epicurean poet and philosopher Philodemus, little is known of this shadowy figure.[34] Philodemus mentions that Neoptolemus treated poet, verse, and poem (or possibly poet, style, and plot[35]) as three separate elements; this may be reflected (if somewhat indirectly) in the *Ars*,

[32] Frischer 1991: 99.
[33] Oliensis 1998: 198.
[34] For some possible further reconstruction of his views, see Asmis 1992.
[35] J. Porter 1995: 104–5.

which does consider all three elements (on whatever interpretation), if not in this strict order or division.[36] Neoptolemus also held that the poet should both charm and benefit his listeners, famously encapsulated at *Ars* 343, *omne tulit punctum qui miscuit utile dulci* ('he who has combined the profitable with the pleasant has gained every vote'). Exhaustive analysis of what can be known about Neoptolemus has got no further than these points,[37] and it seems best to express caution on the details while being clear that the *Ars*, with its strong interest in imitation and drama, is recognizably in the Aristotelian tradition of the *Poetics* which Neoptolemus among many others represented.[38]

This prominence of drama in the *Ars* has often puzzled critics:[39] why should a lyric poet and non-dramatist spend so much time on plays in a work on poetry, especially in a literary period not really known for its drama (Quintilian's comparative catalogue of Roman literature can only muster Varius' *Thyestes* and Ovid's *Medea* for the Augustan years; Quint. 10.1.98). The prominence of the very Greek genre of satyr-play (*Ars* 220–50) is especially mysterious: Wiseman 1988 has argued for a revival of satyr-play under Augustus, but the evidence is limited and unclear. As critics have often contended, the precepts applied by Horace to drama also make sense for his own non-dramatic poetry, for example his material on generic flexibility.[40] In both cases the weight of the Aristotelian tradition is likely to provide part of the solution: Horace carries on the primacy assigned to drama by Peripatetic criticism and by his presumed handbook models, in a tralatician move usual in technical works. We might also think that the *Ars* is happy to return to the classical period of Greek literature and its typical genres, since Augustan Rome could easily be seen by its citizens as a glorious climactic period parallel with fifth-century Athens;[41] recent research has shown some interest in interpreting the *Ars* in the light of other Augustan cultural features, such as developments in visual art.[42] This and other questions will ensure a lively literature on the *Ars* for many years to come.

---

[36] See, for example, Janko 2000: 152–3.
[37] See e.g. Brink 1963: 48–74.
[38] See e.g. Williams 1968: 355; Reinhardt 2013: 504–8.
[39] E.g. Williams 1968: 347.
[40] See Harrison 2007b: 4–6.
[41] Hardie 1997.
[42] Citroni 2008.

VI HORATIAN STYLE AND LITERARY TEXTURE

1. Introduction

In this section I will briefly survey the literature on Horatian poetic style, and then offer some detailed translations and analyses of particular poems from different genres to try to show how Horatian expression works on the page, especially in terms of intertextuality, structural arrangement, and word order.[1] Horace's exceptionally dense and refined poetic texture has been recognized as such since antiquity: Ovid (*Tristia* 4.10.50) refers to Horace's *carmina culta* ('cultured poems'), and Petronius (118.5) to his *curiosa felicitas* ('painstaking felicity of style'), while Quintilian (10.1.96) sees him as *uerbis felicissime audax* ('most felicitously bold in expression'). All these comments are likely to refer primarily to the *Odes*, but can be applied in general to Horace's style through different genres. For the basic facts of Horatian diction and syntax, Bo 1960 remains unrivalled in its sheer level of detail; for more recent overviews and useful scholarly bibliography on Horatian poetic style see the excellent Muecke 1997 and the rest of the major section on style of which it forms the chief part in the *Enciclopedia oraziana* (Mariotti 1996–8), the list of publications in the area up to 2006 by Holzberg,[2] and the helpful survey of the development of Horace's style and metrical practice in Knox 2013. On the metres of the *Odes*, the introductory section in Nisbet and Hubbard 1970 remains a reliable guide;[3] for some more adventurous attempts to relate metre to literary content in Horace see Morgan 2010. The elaborate and expressive word order of the *Odes* is the topic of Nisbet 1999. But the best resources for the analysis of Horatian style and metre are the recent detailed commentaries on Horace's works (listed in Chapter I, section 3), which are closely used in what follows.

---

[1] Translations here are my own.
[2] Holzberg 2007: 126.
[3] Nisbet and Hubbard 1970: xxxviii–xlvi.

2. *Epodes* 4

Lupis et agnis quanta sortito obtigit,
    tecum mihi discordia est,
Hibericis peruste funibus latus
    et crura dura compede.
licet superbus ambules pecunia,   5
    fortuna non mutat genus.
uidesne, sacram metiente te uiam
    cum bis trium ulnarum toga,
ut ora uertat huc et huc euntium
    liberrima indignatio?   10
'sectus flagellis hic triumuiralibus
    praeconis ad fastidium
arat Falerni mille fundi iugera
    et Appiam mannis terit
sedilibusque magnus in primis eques   15
    Othone contempto sedet.
quid attinet tot ora nauium graui
    rostrata duci pondere
contra latrones atque seruilem manum
    hoc, hoc tribuno militum?'

The degree of strife that falls to the lot
    Of wolves and lambs is mine with you,
You with the side burned by Spanish ropes,
    With the calves hardened by slave fetters.
Though you strut about, loftily proud with cash,
    Fortune cannot change breeding.
Can't you see, when you cover the Sacred Way
    Walking with your good nine feet of toga,
How the faces of those who pass, going here and there,
    Are turned to you in the rage of free men?
'This man, once cut by the law officers' whips,
    Until the herald had had enough,
Now ploughs a thousand acres of Falernian farmland
    And wears out the Appian Way with his smart ponies,
And as a mighty knight sits in the front seats,
    Scorning Otho and his law.
What's the point of so many ships' prows,
    Beaked with heavy weight, being launched
Against those brigands and their band of slaves
    When this, this man is a military tribune?'

The political and cultural references in this poem are excellently treated
by Watson 2003: here I want to focus more on diction. The enmity of

wolves and lambs with which the poem begins recalls Achilles' famous declaration of hostility to Hector at *Iliad* 22.262–4 ('just as wolves and lambs cannot have a common mind, but always intend evil to one another, so it is not possible for you and me to be friends'). The Homeric epic model is brought down to the lower level of the iambic genre by its context – not an exchange between heroes but one between lower characters – and this may suggest that the poet and his target might be more on the same level than is at first apparent: commentators have noted the disturbing similarity between the ex-slave and Horace (servile background, now a knight and a military tribune owing to civil war disturbances).[4] The language is mixed: *discordia* can be lofty, going back to Ennius and Lucretius, but the adverb *sortito* and the verb *obtingere* are colloquial and ordinary, found only in Plautus and prose authors before Horace.[5]

Note the expressive word order: the hostility between the two enemies is clear in the juxtaposed pronouns *tecum mihi*, and the identifying elements of other place-names are put up front for emphasis (7: *sacram ... uiam* for the normal *uiam ... sacram*; 13: *Falerni ... fundi* for the normal *fundus ... Falernus*), stressing that this interloper is taking over the best of Rome and Italy. The emphatic *liberrima indignatio* (10) is similarly delayed and pithily presented in a single iambic tetrameter, just like the gnomic maxim *fortuna non mutat genus* (6).

The language of the epode makes clear reference to Catullus, an important predecessor for Horace's iambics:[6] the picture of the parvenu walking proudly around Rome and his sudden acquisition of an agricultural estate both recall Catullus' similar arriviste Mamurra (29.6–7: *et ille nunc* superbus *et superfluens* / perambulabit *omnium cubilia* ['and he now, proud and overflowing, will wander through the beds of all']; 115.1: *Mentula habet iuxta triginta* iugera *prati* ['Dick has some three hundred acres of meadowland']; cf. 114). Another important model here is Lucretius' similar attack on contemporary materialism: the rich man rushing along the Appian Way with his fashionable ponies (*manni*) picks up the similar picture of the speedy elite member at *De rerum natura* 3.1064: *currit agens* mannos *ad uillam praecipitanter* ('speeds along, driving his smart little ponies to his villa, all in a rush').

[4] Cf. Watson 2003: 150–2.
[5] *Sortito* is only otherwise found in verse at Silius 10.593.
[6] See Heyworth 2001; Putnam 2006.

The imagined speech of the passers-by adds a vivid element to the poem and confirms the poet's judgement as generally shared at Rome: it also allows a move from second-person address to third-person description of the target, a variation neatly placed in the centre of the poem, a point where Horatian poems often pivot in various ways. The speech naturally has a colloquial air, but is still self-consciously artistic: note how the name of one legal officer is followed directly in the next line by another (*triumualibus / praeconis*), displaced from its natural position to allow this effect. Likewise, in line 15 the interlaced word order seems to express the sense of the line – the parvenu sits in great state in the midst of the front equestrian rows at the theatre, just as *magnus* is enclosed within the phrase describing the prestigious seating area (*sedilibus ... in primis*), and the expression referring to the weighty ships provides another example of complex poetic word order in lines 17–18 (more natural Latin might read *quid attinet tot ora nauium graui pondere rostrata duci*). The repeated pronoun *hoc, hoc* rhetorically expresses the emotion of the speaker, as often in the invective of the *Epodes*.[7]

3. *Odes* 2.6

> Septimi, Gadis aditure mecum et
> Cantabrum indoctum iuga ferre nostra et
> barbaras Syrtis, ubi Maura semper
>   aestuat unda,
> Tibur Argeo positum colono   5
> sit meae sedes utinam senectae,
> sit modus lasso maris et uiarum
>   militiaeque.
> unde si Parcae prohibent iniquae,
> dulce pellitis ouibus Galaesi   10
> flumen et regnata petam Laconi
>   rura Phalantho.
> ille terrarum mihi praeter omnis
> angulus ridet, ubi non Hymetto
> mella decedunt uiridique certat   15
>   baca Venafro,
> uer ubi longum tepidasque praebet
> Iuppiter brumas et amicus Aulon

---

[7] Watson 2003: 171 compares 5.53, 6.11, 7.1, 14.6, 17.1, and 17.7.

fertili Baccho minimum Falernis
     inuidet uuis.   20
ille te mecum locus et beatae
postulant arces; ibi tu calentem
debita sparges lacrima fauillam
     uatis amici.

Septimius, who would go with me to visit Cadiz
And the Cantabrians not yet taught to bear our yoke,
Or the wild Syrtes, where the African swell
     Seethes unrelenting,
May Tibur, set down by an Argive founder,
Be the place of rest for my old age,
May it be the end point for one who is tired of sea,
     Journeys, and service!
But if the Fates' unkindness deny this wish,
I will seek out the Galaesus river, sweet water
For leather-jacketed sheep, and the fields once ruled by
     Spartan Phalanthus.
That corner of the world smiles to me above all other,
Where the honey yields no place to Hymettus,
Where the olive-fruit is able to compete
     With green Venafrum,
Where Jupiter grants a lengthy spring
And warm midwinters, and the Aulon,
Friend to fertile Bacchus, feels no envy of
     Grapes of Falerii.
That is the place that calls you and me
With its happy citadels: there you will scatter
With due tears the still-warm ashes of
     Your friend the poet.

The four-line stanzaic metres (here the Sapphic stanza) of most of Horace's *Odes* are an important element in their poetic texture, since they create internal structural building blocks which can be variously exploited. This poem turns in the middle, after three of the six stanzas, as often in the *Odes*.[8] The first half is full of movement from the wild to the tame, presenting possible extreme exotic destinations and then reaching the peaceful and mild Tarentum (the city of Spartan foundation) via Tibur, while the second half is a static encomiastic account of an imaginary life in residence at Tarentum. The second and third stanzas balance each other in each containing a brief account of alternative

---

[8] See Harrison 2004.

Italian destinations, the 'suburban' Tibur and the deep southern Tarentum, while the fourth and fifth stanzas stand together as a unit more fully praising the climatic advantages of Tarentum. The first and last (sixth) stanzas are linked by ring composition, both focusing on Septimius' extreme loyalty as a friend, shown in his readiness to travel with the poet to the ends of the earth and to attend to his funeral rites; and the concluding Italian 'home' location of Tarentum clearly contrasts with the distant 'away' locations of the first stanza, providing a closure which is quieter and less dramatic than the opening.

This structure is carefully articulated by verbal signposts. The first and second stanzas stress the two balancing place-names by initial location (1 *Septimi, Gadis*; 5 *Tibur*) while succeeding stanzas are linked by paired relatives (9 *unde*; 16 *ubi*), and by repeated demonstrative pronouns (13 *ille*; 21 *ille*), all again carefully initially placed. As often, place-names provide extended poetic colour. In this poem, as in *Epodes* 4, allusion to Catullus, the great lyric poet of the previous generation, can be seen. The poem's opening theme of perilous possible journey into theatres of war and far-distant lands as a token of friendship recalls Catullus 11, a poem in the same Sapphic metre, the opening stanzas of which are evoked by Horace here (both first stanzas end with the word *unda*).[9] In his poem Catullus had combined distant historic Eastern locations associated with the achievements of Alexander and places recalling more contemporary campaigns in the 50s BCE (Crassus in Parthia, Caesar in Britain), and Horace follows this, linking the contemporary Cantabrian battlefields of northern Spain with the legendary Syrtes. West has rightly suggested that Horace's ode provides a calmer and more mature response to Catullus' passionate request, where the friends addressed are asked to deliver a devastating message to the poet's *puella* rather than invited to share his retirement.[10] Friendship is about lifelong companionship rather than momentary support in an erotic crisis.

Poetic language is as important here as structural effects and literary intertextuality. The first stanza picks out environments which are distant, forbidding, or actually hostile as potentially testing destinations for Septimius' loyal companionship, and the three destinations are described at increasing length, forming an ascending tricolon (a list of three with the last element longest) linked by *et ... et*. The phrase

[9] See Nisbet and Hubbard 1978: 97.
[10] West 1998: 42–3.

Cantabrum indoctum iuga ferre nostra is especially rich: the collective singular used of the enemy and *noster* of 'our' Romans strongly evoke the language of historians,[11] while *indoctum* and *iuga ferre* (pointing to yoking bulls) suggest the stupidity and animalistic character of Rome's barbarian enemies.

The manipulation of proper names and adjectives is again prominent here. The foreign locations or peoples *Gadis*, *Cantabrum*, and *Maura* are all put at the earliest possible point in their clause, against natural Latin word order, while *Syrtis* is put as close as possible to *Maura*, reflecting the fact that both locations belong to North Africa. Each of stanzas 2–5 has two different place-names or geographical adjectives, while stanza 1 has four and stanza 6 has none; furthermore, in each of stanzas 2–5, one of the two place-names is Latin (*Tibur*, *Galaesi*, *Venafro*, *Falernis*), while the other is Greek (*Argeo*, *Laconi*, *Hymetto*, *Aulon*). This especially suits the cultural environment of Tarentum in the heavily Hellenized deep south of Italy. Likewise, the two balancing destination cities of Tibur and Tarentum are described in a wholly balanced way by reference to their Greek founders, even with matching constructions of participles and dative of agents: *Tibur Argeo positum colono* (5) is closely mirrored by *regnata … Laconi / rura Phalantho* (11–12). Similarly, the rival place-names of *Hymetto* and *Venafrum* are carefully placed in appropriately opposing positions at either end of their clause in 14–16.

Personification is a notable technique here: in 14 the charms of Tarentum are said to smile on the poet (*ridet*), while in 14–16 products are poetically said to compete directly with places, using nouns not the expected topographical adjectives, with the adjective 'green' transferred from the olive to its origin in Venafrum. The verbs *decedunt … certat* ('yield to', 'compete') are striking, perhaps evoking Roman aristocrats jockeying for political or social position. There is also a nice variation between two poetic uses of number in 15–16, with *mella* a poetic plural and *baca* a collective singular, both usages found in Virgil's *Georgics*, which may be echoed thematically here in this list of Italian products recalling the so-called 'praise of Italy' at *Georgics* 2.136–76.

The short last line of the Sapphic stanza (the adonaean) is clearly used to good effect here: the important term *militiaeque*, expressing exhaustion with campaigning and perhaps an end to the need for it

---

[11] Nisbet and Hubbard 1970: 214; *OLD*, s.v. *noster* 7.

in civil war, is reserved for this emphatic position in the second stanza, filling the whole line in a rare effect reserved elsewhere in Horace for the stressing of proper names (cf. *Odes* 1.12.40: *Fabriciumque*; 1.30.8: *Mercuriusque*). The adonaeans of the third and fourth stanzas are perfectly balanced in shape, with a disyllabic common noun followed by a trisyllabic name, with matching vowel endings (12: *rura Phalantho*; 16: *baca Venafro*), while that of the last stanza provides an epistolary-style signature to the poem as well as an implicit statement of its motivation (24: *uatis amici*). The poem thus returns to its initial theme, marked by the formal ring composition between the opening of the first stanza and the last: *ille te mecum locus* (21) clearly picks up the first line's *Septimi, Gadis aditure mecum* with its focus on the addressee, its specification of a place, and its suggestion of a shared journey of friendship.

4. *Epistles* 1.11

> *Quid tibi uisa Chios, Bullati, notaque Lesbos,*
> *quid concinna Samos, quid Croesi regia Sardis,*
> *Zmyrna quid et Colophon? Maiora minoraue fama?*
> *cunctane prae Campo et Tiberino flumine sordent?*
> *An uenit in uotum Attalicis ex urbibus una?*   5
> *An Lebedum laudas odio maris atque uiarum?*
> *Scis Lebedus quid sit: Gabiis desertior atque*
> *Fidenis uicus; tamen illic uiuere uellem,*
> *oblitusque meorum, obliuiscendus et illis,*
> *Neptunum procul e terra spectare furentem.*   10
> *Sed neque qui Capua Romam petit, imbre lutoque*
> *aspersus uolet in caupona uiuere; nec qui*
> *frigus collegit, furnos et balnea laudat*
> *ut fortunatam plene praestantia uitam;*
> *nec si te ualidus iactauerit Auster in alto,*   15
> *idcirco nauem trans Aegaeum mare uendas.*
> *Incolumi Rhodos et Mytilene pulchra facit quod*
> *paenula solstitio, campestre niualibus auris,*
> *per brumam Tiberis, Sextili mense caminus.*
> *Dum licet ac uoltum seruat Fortuna benignum,*   20
> *Romae laudetur Samos et Chios et Rhodos absens.*
> *Tu quamcumque deus tibi fortunauerit horam*
> *grata sume manu neu dulcia differ in annum,*
> *ut quocumque loco fueris uixisse libenter*
> *te dicas; nam si ratio et prudentia curas,*   25
> *non locus effusi late maris arbiter aufert,*

caelum, non animum mutant, qui trans mare currunt.
Strenua nos exercet inertia: nauibus atque
quadrigis petimus bene uiuere. Quod petis, hic est,
est Ulubris, animus si te non deficit aequus.   30

How did Chios seem to you, Bullatius, and famous Lesbos,
And pretty Samos, and the palace of Croesus at Sardis,
What of Smyrna and Colophon – better or worse than their fame?
Or are they all as dirt beside the Campus and the Tiber's stream?
Or does one of the cities of Attalus surface in your prayers,
Or do you commend Lebedus, now sick of sea and travel?
'You know what Lebedus is, a mere village, emptier
Than Gabii or Fidenae – yet there I'd like to live,
And forgetting my friends, to be forgotten by them,
Watch Neptune raging at safe distance from the shore.'
But he who makes for Rome from Capua, spattered
With rain and mud, would not want to *live* in an inn,
And even he who has caught a cold does not praise stoves and hot baths
As the only purveyors of the truly happy life.
Nor would you, if a strong south wind should toss you on the deep,
Sell off your ship across the Aegean as a consequence.
For one in good health, Rhodes and fair Mytilene
Do the same as a cloak in midsummer, a light tunic in snowy blasts,
A Tiber dip in midwinter, a furnace in the month of August.
While you can and Fortune keeps her features kind,
Let Samos and Chios and Rhodes be praised at Rome for their distance.
Whatever hour god has kindly bestowed on you,
Grasp it with grateful hand and don't postpone pleasure for another season:
This way you can say that wherever you were
You lived most gladly: for if reason and good sense,
Not a place which commands a wide spread of sea, banish cares,
Those who speed across the sea change their climate, not their temper.
Our energetic sloth gives us a workout: by ship and chariot
We seek for the good life. But what you seek is here,
Here at Ulubrae, if you have sufficient steady mind.

The style of the hexameter epistles is looser and more relaxed than that
of the *Odes*, and closer to the *Epodes*, but still full of artistry. Here, once
again, place-names are carefully positioned, with a list of three islands
followed by a list of three cities: *Chios, Lesbos, Samos,* and *Sardis* all
stand either at the main caesura of the hexameter, at its formal centre,
or at its end, *Zmyrna* at the start of the line, and *Colophon* again at the
caesura. Note too the artistic variation of expression in the list of
names: Chios has no epithet, Lesbos and Samos a single one, Sardis
a phrase in apposition, then Zmyrna and Colophon no epithet. These

places have resonance for the connoisseur of Greek literature: Chios was often seen as the birthplace of Homer, while Lesbos was that of Sappho and Alcaeus, and Samos the origin of the epic poet Choerilus and the epigrammatist Asclepiades; Sardis was the capital of Croesus, whose defeat and capture there by Cyrus is a famous episode in Herodotus (1.81–90), Zmyrna the home of the bucolic poet Bion, Colophon of the elegiac and hexameter poet Nicander. Horace as poet perhaps asks his friend about places with particular literary connections. There are other poetically effective juxtapositions of proper names: *Capua Romam* (11) fittingly places together a journey's starting place and its destination, while *Tiberis, Sextili* (19) nicely cuts across two clauses to suggest that river swimming is in fact a real pleasure in high summer.

Lucretius, an important precedent for Horace's hexameter moralizing,[12] also features here, as in *Epode* 4. The elegant line 10 – *Neptunum procul e terra spectare furentem* – is Lucretian in both style and content. Its two highly poetic features – the metonymy of 'god for thing' Neptune = 'sea', and a line-enclosing noun–adjective/participle pair – are both found in Lucretius (2.472: Neptuni *corpus acerbum*; 1.9: placatumque *nitet diffuso lumine* caelum[13]), and recalls Lucretius' penchant for the famous one-line *sententia* (rhetorical maxim): compare, for example, Lucretius 1.101: *tantum religio potuit suadere malorum* ('so great an evil could superstition urge'), another memorable moral notion encapsulated in a single hexameter. This technique is in fact common in the *Epistles* to highlight key ideas.[14] The line's theme, the idea of calmly contemplating dangers at sea from the safety of land as a metaphor for mental peace, clearly recalls the famous opening of Lucretius' second book (2.1–2): *Suaue, mari magno turbantibus aequora uentis / e terra magnum alterius* spectare *laborem* ('pleasant it is, when winds could trouble on the great expanse of the ocean, to gaze at another's mighty tribulation from the shore'). Similarly Lucretian is the picture of the man who vainly seeks relief from anxiety and boredom in travel, picking up both the image of rapid equine transit (29: *quadrigis*) and its moral futility from Lucretius 3.1063–4, already alluded to in the *manni* of *Epodes* 4.14 (see above). Meanwhile the

---

[12] See Freudenburg 1993: 19.
[13] See further Pearce 1966: 162.
[14] See Harrison 1995c.

famous one-line *sententia* of 27, *caelum non animum mutant qui trans mare currunt*, once again makes use of a Lucretian technique (see above).

Pointed verbal style is still evident in the more relaxed texture of the *Epistles*. In line 4 we find the juxtaposition *flumine sordent*, a neat oxymoron as river water (*flumine*) naturally cleans rather than dirties, the root meaning of *sordent*; a similar oxymoron is found in 28: *strenua ... inertia*. Such expressions are a central part of Horace's style.[15] In line 9 there are two varied forms of the same verb in a neat and pithy expression in a chiastic order, each time with a balancing complement referring to the same group of people as both subjects and objects of forgetting (*oblitusque meorum obliuiscendus et illis*). The word order of line 21 postpones the crucial *absens* as a neat sting in the tail: 'at Rome you can praise all places – provided you don't go there', just as the last word of the whole poem (*aequus*) sums up its doctrine: that equanimity is the most important virtue.

---

[15] See West 1973.

VII RECEPTIONS OF HORACE

1. Introduction

The study of classical reception, the influence of classical texts and culture in later times and works, has been one of the biggest growth areas in classical scholarship in the twenty-first century. There has been considerable discussion of how classical reception is to be defined: for some orientation see Hardwick 2003, Martindale and Thomas 2006, and Hardwick and Stray 2008. Most would now view it as a kind of dialogue between classical original(s) and later work(s) which use, appropriate, or modify the original(s), and emphasize the need to understand both cultural contexts as well as remembering our own situatedness. When we look at, say, Ben Jonson's reception of Horace there are three contexts involved: ourselves in our own period and culture, Jonson in his, and Horace in his, and we are in effect reading Jonson reading Horace. In a sense, all that classical scholars do is a form of reception, as they are always inevitably receiving classical texts in the particular light of their own culture and characteristics, whether or not they articulate this explicitly. One strand of classical reception is connected with translation: a translation is never a neutral rendering of a text but is always necessarily coloured by the culture and ideology of the translator. Another is connected with literary imitation or adaptation: classical works can be very effectively recast in a new cultural context. As we shall see, Horace has been richly received in both these ways, and in others.

2. Surveys

Among older works, Showerman 1922 provides a brief but wide-ranging survey which looks at receptions of Horace from antiquity to its own time, while the two volumes of Stemplinger (1906, 1921) are more ambitious accounts of Horace's European reception, especially of the *Odes*. The modern era of work begins with the bimillennium of Horace's death in 1992/3, which stimulated a number of important publications. These include the rich material on the reception of

Horace from the medieval to the modern period and in different countries in the 1996–8 *Enciclopedia oraziana*[1] and the reception chapters in
Ludwig 1993a; two useful collections are Krasser and Schmidt 1996,
focusing particularly on reception in German, and especially Martindale
and Hopkins 1993 on UK reception from the Renaissance to the twentieth century, in many ways the first application of modern ideas about
reception to the poet. Two of the three current Horace handbooks have
substantial sections on reception, now the most convenient points of
departure on this topic;[2] a wide perspective is also offered by a recent conference volume which covers receptions of Horace from antiquity to the
contemporary period.[3] A fine anthology of translations into English and
some adaptations is to be found in Carne-Ross and Haynes 1996.

3. Antiquity and the Middle Ages

The reception of Horace in antiquity is a rich field, especially in terms
of his influence on later lyric poetry: Tarrant 2007 maps out some of
the territory, but an important link is that with the late antique
Prudentius, the most extensive user of Horace's lyric metres in the
new Christian context and a major channel from Horace to medieval
hymnography.[4] For the hexameter poetry, Barchiesi 2001d (see also
Ingleheart 2010) has made a fascinating argument that Ovid's long
epistle to Augustus (*Tristia* 2) reacts to Horace's similar poetic letter
(*Epistles* 2.1); Horatian satire is also naturally important for Persius
and Juvenal, who react with and against their famous generic
predecessor.[5]

   The Carolingian period (see again Tarrant 2007) saw copying of all
the poems and imitations of Horatian lyric by some of its leading poets
(Walahfrid Strabo and Paul the Deacon). In the later medieval period
Horace could be referred to as 'satirist' by Dante (*Inferno* 4.89: *Orazio
satiro*), but all his works seem to have been widely read.[6] A large range
of introductions and *accessus* to the poet is available in manuscripts of

[1] Mariotti 1996–8: iii.81–612.
[2] Harrison 2007a; Davis 2010a.
[3] Houghton and Wyke 2009.
[4] See e.g. Palmer 1989; Pucci 1991; Flammini 2007–8; Longobardi 2010.
[5] See, for example, Rudd 1976: 54–83; Freudenburg 2001.
[6] For a brief account of the surviving manuscripts, see Munk Olsen 1996. For surveys of his
influence, see Quint 1988; Friis-Jensen 1993, 2007.

the period, plus glosses by readers, which show clearly how and why
Horace was read at the time,[7] and the use of Horatian imitation by
poets such as the eleventh-century Alphanus of Salerno and the twelfth-
century 'Archpoet' and Metellus of Tegernsee has been a topic of
recent scholarship.[8] Petrarch wrote a brief Horatian ode in the second
asclepiad stanza of *Odes* 1.5 (*Carmina* 23) and a splendid letter to
Horace himself in 138 minor asclepiad lines (*Familiares* 24.10), the
metre of *Odes* 1.1, 3.30, and 4.8.[9] Interesting too are the medieval
texts of Horace presented with neumes (musical notation),[10] which
have been argued by some to preserve a performance tradition which
is continuous from antiquity.[11]

4. The Renaissance to 1660

The renewal of learning and the invention of printing led not only
to many learned editions of Horace's works, such as those of
Christoforo Landino in Italy (1482) and Denys Lambin in France
(1561 and 1567), but also to many more imitations of his poetry all
over Europe, especially in Italy.[12] Until the middle of the fifteenth century, few had followed Petrarch's limited attempts to imitate the easier
Horatian lyric metres: more serious imitation was a fitting challenge for
the great humanists of the Quattrocento. The texts of many of these
Neo-Latin poets are now becoming much more widely available,
both via the fine *I Tatti Renaissance Library* series of parallel texts and
translations[13] and in online databases,[14] enlarging their readership
beyond specialists in a period where the study of Neo-Latin itself is a
growing discipline.[15]

A major early figure is Giovanni Pontano (1426–1503), who wrote
sixteen odes in Sapphics in Naples in the mid-1450s, later published

[7] Friis-Jensen 1993.
[8] Friis-Jensen 1993; Harrison 1997; Friis-Jensen 2007.
[9] Ludwig 1993b; Houghton 2009.
[10] Ziolkowski 2000; Wälli 2002.
[11] Lyons 2007.
[12] For surveys, see Ludwig 1993b; McGann 2007.
[13] See <http://www.hup.harvard.edu/collection.php?cpk=1145>.
[14] For two of the most important, see, for poets working in Italy, *Poeti d'Italia in lingua latina*,
<http://www.mqdq.it/mqdq/poetiditalia/indice_autori_alfa.jsp?scelta=AZ&path=autori>, and, more
generally (and especially for poets working in the UK), the vast resources of the Birmingham
Philological Museum, <http://www.philological.bham.ac.uk/>.
[15] See especially Knight and Tilg 2014.

in his *Lyra* (1501) and more Horatian in form than content (they include an ode to his wife and a pair of poems exchanged between Polyphemus and Galatea). Francesco Filelfo (1426–81) explored Horatian lyric in a wider range of metres in his fifty *Odes* in five books (one more than Horace), which seem to have been completed in the 1450s.[16] These often long lyric poems present a kind of autobiography, working through the concerns of Filelfo's career – just rule, war peace, love, the intellectual life; the first poems of the first, middle, and last books are addressed to Charles VII of France, and those in between address various individuals and topics significant to the poet and his career. Filelfo uses a good number of Horatian metres (including asclepiadic measures) but has not mastered the whole range; he is able to write in Sapphic stanzas but not in the more intricate Alcaics, and has a fair amount of (less ambitious) elegiacs and hexameters.

In the next generation, the great Angelo Poliziano (1454–94), a fine composer in hexameters, in his *Odae* likewise managed only Sapphics and some asclepiadic metres, including (following Petrarch) an ode to Horace himself (in asclepiads),[17] but not Alcaics. The three books of epigrams of his enemy Jacopo Sannazaro (1456–1530), author of the influential Italian *Arcadia* and another splendid Latin poet, similarly have only poems in Sapphics from Horace's metres, including one (2.36) to a spring at Mergellina which must echo the asclepiadic *Odes* 3.13.[18] The earliest master of the full spectrum of Horatian lyric metres is Sannazaro's friend Michael Marullus (1458–1500), the Greek-born, Italian-educated soldier and poet, who in the 1490s composed in Alcaics as well as Sapphics and some other complex measures, especially in the noble cosmic hymns of his 1497 *Hymni naturales*.[19]

In the sixteenth century, polished imitations of Horatian lyrics were widely published across Europe. In the German-speaking countries Conrad Celtis (1459–1508) wrote four books of *Odes*, one of *Epodes*, and a *Carmen saeculare* (published 1513), brilliantly imitating Horace on a micro- and macro-level.[20] This initiated a series of German Horatian lyric poets in the sixteenth and seventeenth centuries.[21] In

---

[16] See the helpful new edition in Robin 2009.

[17] Conveniently found in Ludwig 1993b.

[18] For an edition of his Latin poems, see Putnam 2009.

[19] See the recent edition of his poems in Fantazzi 2012, and the study of Lefèvre and Schäfer 2008.

[20] For texts, see Schäfer 2008; Forster 2011. For discussion, see Auhagen et al. 2000.

[21] See Schäfer 1976; Gruber 1997.

France, Jean Salmon Macrin (1490–1557) became known as the 'French Horace', publishing a wide range of Latin lyrics, especially in his *Carminum libri IV* of 1530, which included a Sapphic ode to Horace himself.[22] The works (1541) of the Dutch-born peripatetic Joannes Secundus (1511–36), best known for his Catullan *Basia*, contain a book of elegant Horatian odes.[23] Both Macrin and Secundus were influential on the major French lyric poets of the later sixteenth century. In Spain, the important vernacular poet Garcilaso de le Vega (1503–36) composed three fine Horatian odes,[24] while Jan Kochanowski (1530–84), often regarded as the founder of Polish vernacular verse, wrote a number of fine Horatian Latin odes in his *Lyricorum libellus* (1580).[25]

One of the most able imitators of Horace was the Scot George Buchanan (1506–82), who spent much of his life in France and eventually returned to Scotland for a top-level academic and political career, including acting as tutor to both Mary Queen of Scots and James VI/I.[26] He composed both fine odes in Horace's manner on political events and a virtuoso and much-imitated set of psalm-paraphrases in the lyric metres of the *Odes*, with occasional elements from the *Epodes*, thus combining humanistic Horatianism with Protestant piety.[27] This led to a fine tradition of Horatianism in Scotland, evident in the anthology *Delitiae poetarum Scotorum* (1637), currently the subject of a major research project, which included Buchanan alongside religious Horatian odes by Andrew Melville (1545–1622).[28]

Two highly talented neo-Horatians were Jesuits. The German Alsatian Jakob Balde (1604–68)[29] like others matched Horace's four books of *Odes* in his 1643 *Libri lyricorum* (mostly on moralizing religious subjects)[30] and published a single book of *Epodes*,[31] as well as a book of

---

[22] Printed in Ludwig 1993b. See also Ford 1997; Soubeille 1998. For other French Horation odes of the sixteenth century, see Schmitz 1994.

[23] For a study of its erotic poems, see Schäfer 2004.

[24] Texts at <http://www.thelatinlibrary.com/garcilaso.html>; English discussion in Lumsden 1947.

[25] Discussion in Glomski 1987; texts available at <http://neolatina.bj.uj.edu.pl>.

[26] See McFarlane 1981.

[27] For a splendid recent edition see Green 2011. For discussions, see Green 2000, 2009; Harrison 2012.

[28] Available at <http://www.gla.ac.uk/schools/humanities/research/historyresearch/researchprojects/delitiaepoetarumscotorum/>.

[29] See Thill 1991, 1993.

[30] For a partial modern text and commentary see Thill 1987.

[31] See Winter 2002.

Sylvae which included many poems in lyric metres.[32] The fluent moralizing Horatian odes of Maciej Kazimierz Sarbiewski (1595–1640), known as the 'Polish Horace', many written in Rome in praise of Urban VIII, were widely read and much imitated in European vernacular literature, especially in English.[33] We have also recently been reminded that a limited group of women as well as men read Horace in this period.[34]

English translations and imitations of Horace began to emerge in the mid-sixteenth century. The complete hexameter poems were translated by Thomas Drant (1567), while odd odes were translated by the major poets the Earl of Surrey and Sir Philip Sidney.[35] An important figure here is Ben Jonson, whose engagement with Horace encompassed translation, imitation, and presenting him as a character on stage in his 1601 play *Poetaster*.[36] Sir Richard Fanshawe's translation of selected parts of Horace (1652) was soon followed by the first complete English translation, by several hands, published by Alexander Brome (1666); notable imitations can be found in Marvell and Cowley.[37]

5. 1660–1800

In the UK, this period saw the growth of English satire under Dryden and Pope, often departing from and using Horace's hexameter poetry: for recent useful surveys see Money 2007, Hooley 2012, and Sowerby 2012. Pope's detailed imitations of Horatian satires are particularly rich, and Dryden's splendid version of *Odes* 3.29 is notable.[38] Important translations of Horace were published by Thomas Creech (1684, much criticized) and Christopher Smart, whose prose translation of 1754 was a school standard for two centuries but whose verse translation of 1767 was long unjustly neglected;[39] the most durable from this period is that of Philip Francis (1749, much reprinted). Neo-Latin Horatian imitation remained strong in this period:

[32] See Lefèvre and Schäfer 2010.
[33] For a selection, see Thill 1995. See also Schäfer 2006; Fordoński and Urbański 2010.
[34] Stevenson 2009.
[35] See Burrow 1993; J. Scodel 2010: 213–20.
[36] See Moul 2010.
[37] For Marvell, see Nuttall 1993; for Cowley, see Hopkins 1993.
[38] For Pope, see Stack 1985; Rudd 1994: 61–90. For Dryden, see Gillespie 1993.
[39] See now Williamson 1996.

Poetarum Scotorum musae sacrae (1739), a successor anthology to the *Delitiae poetarum Scotorum* (1637), included Horatian lyric metres in parts of verse paraphrases of the Song of Solomon by John Ker (d. 1741) and of the Book of Job by William Hog (d. 1702; better known for his 1690 translation into Latin hexameters of Milton's *Paradise Lost*), while the Oxford poet Anthony Alsop (d. 1726) produced some remarkable Horatian lyrics.[40] In general, the English literature of the eighteenth century, both prose and verse, is saturated in Horatian imitation.[41]

Elsewhere in Europe, the key text of the French classicizing period was the expanded version of the *Ars poetica* by Nicholas Boileau (1674), which exercised much influence on Pope and Dryden (see above) as well as in France. In Germany, Friedrich von Hagendorn (d. 1754) was the best-known representative of a group of poets who used Horace to recreate lyric poetry in the eighteenth century; Christoph Martin Wieland's translation of Horace's hexameter poetry (1786) is also notable, while Herder wrote an essay (1802) on reading Horace and Lessing a defence (1754) of the poet's moral character.[42] In Italy, the dramatist and opera librettist Pietro Metastasio produced a version of the *Ars poetica* (1749).[43]

6. 1800–1900

Though the English Romantics might revolt against the tyranny of being taught Horace at school, they still admired him, a tension which comes out well in Byron's famous lines, motivated by the sight of Soracte in Italy and consequent recall of *Odes* 1.9: 'Then farewell Horace, whom I hated so, / Not for thy faults, but mine'.[44] The Romantic link of literature and landscape is also seen in Wordsworth's desire to explore 'Sabine vales' following 'a wish / To meet the shade of Horace by the side / Of his Bandusian fount', combining an allusion to *Odes* 3.4 with one to *Odes* 3.13 in his *Memorials of*

---

[40] For introductions to Neo-Latin Horation imitation see Money 1998: 1–53; Money 2007. For Alsop, see Money 1998.

[41] See Hopkins and Martindale 2012, and the still useful collection of data in Goad 1918.

[42] On von Hagendorn, see Schmidt 2002a; on Wieland, Curran 1995; on Herder, Schmidt 2003–4; on Lessing, Hamilton 2001.

[43] See Orlando 1993.

[44] *Childe Harold*, Canto IV (1919), line 77.

a Tour of Italy (1837). Keats, generally more interested in Hellenic culture, could echo Horace in the opening of one of his most famous
poems, 'Ode to a Nightingale', I.1–4: 'My heart aches, and a drowsy
numbness pains / my senses' clearly echoes *Epodes* 14.1–4, in its initial
position as well as in its theme. For some basic data on English poets'
imitation of Horace across the nineteenth century see Thayer 1916.

Horace was a key part of UK elite education in the Victorian period
and served as a model for the English gentleman in various ways.[45]
Among translations, John Conington, the Corpus Professor of Latin
at Oxford, produced versions of the *Odes* (1863) and the hexameter
works (1870), the former showing the influence of Sir Walter Scott,
while Sir Theodore Martin, biographer of Prince Albert, translated
both the *Odes* (1860) and then the complete works (1881). The translation of Horace seems to have been particularly favoured by retired
statesmen, perhaps imitating the poet's famous literary *otium* or leisure:
Lord Lytton's version of the *Odes* of 1869 was reprinted several times,
and the *Odes* were also translated by W. E. Gladstone at the end of his
life (1894). The undoubtedly central place of Horace in Victorian literary culture did not prevent criticism. Matthew Arnold in 'On the
Modern Element in Literature' (1857) sees the 'gentlemanly' Horace
as 'inadequate', lacking key Victorian virtues and representing the
middlebrow taste of the Philistine bourgeoisie whom Arnold hoped
to direct to the superior joys of Hellenism. Nevertheless, the younger
Arnold had indulged in Horatian pastiche in his 'Horatian Echo'
(1847), which addresses a friend advising him not to worry about politics in a clear echo of the opening of *Odes* 2.11. Arnold's friend Arthur
Hugh Clough likewise made some use of both the *Odes* and the *Epistles*
in his epistolary *Amours de voyage* (1858), which ends with an envoi
plainly echoing the closing poem of Horace's *Epistles* 1 (1.20).

The practice of Horatian pastiche, like that of Horatian translation,
became extensive in the nineteenth century, with some interesting
adaptations to Victorian social and intellectual contexts. The most distinguished example of these *vers de société* is Tennyson's 'To the Rev. F.
D. Maurice', which, like Arnold's 'Horatian Echo', neatly inserts real
current affairs into the literary frame.[46] Thackeray's version of *Odes*
1.38, Horace's address to his wine-pourer urging simple party prac-
tices, neatly replaces the dubious boy with an address to 'Lucy',

---

[45] On elite education, see Gaisser 1994; on Horace as model, see Harrison 2007c.
[46] See Rudd 2005: 177–90.

perhaps a maid. The enormously (and deservedly) popular 'version' of the medieval Persian *Rubaiyat of Omar Khayyam* (1859) by Tennyson's friend Edward Fitzgerald, 'the Bible of Victorian agnosticism', has more than a touch of Horace about it, using Horatian-style quatrain stanzas and a first-person, world-weary, ageing narrator.

Horatian influence was so general that it could reach into the most unlikely literary corners of Victorian England.[47] The most famous poem of the 1890s, by Ernest Dowson (1867–1900), shows Horace transposed into the perhaps notably un-Horatian arena of low and haunting obsessive physical passion: *Non sum qualis eram bonae sub regno Cynarae* (published 1896) appropriates *Odes* 4.1.4 as its title ('I am not the man I was under the sway of the kindly Cinara'). A rather more conventional version of Horace, though perhaps with some erotic undertones, is to be found in the well-known version of *Odes* 4.7 published almost simultaneously by A. E. Housman in 1897.[48]

7. Modern Horaces

Quite different was the use of Horace in the Edwardian/Georgian period by Rudyard Kipling and Sir Henry Newbolt, showing the enlistment of Horace in British imperial ideology. Kipling wrote perhaps the most famous English parody of Horace's *Odes* in 'A Translation' (1917), while the story 'Regulus' (1917) in the school collection *Stalky and Co.* examines the imperial lessons of *Odes* 3.5.[49] Newbolt, poet of empire, produced a version of *Odes* 1.7, 'Laudabunt alii' (1907), in which Horace's Tibur is metamorphosed into Newbolt's native Devon. At the zenith of the British Empire, Horatian imitation was a natural vehicle for nationalistic poetry. This was famously undermined in the next generation by Wilfred Owen, who in 'Dulce et Decorum Est' (1917) cited in a poem's title and refuted in its climax Horace's famous declaration (*Odes* 3.12.13: *dulce et decorum est pro patria mori*) that death for one's country was both sweet and glorious.

The continuing central role of Horace in Anglophone elite education until the 1960s ensured further allusion and appropriation in modern British and American poetry. Both in the 1930s and at the end of his

[47] For a survey, see Vance 1997: 175–93.
[48] See now Gaskin 2013 for Housman's engagement with and similarities to Horace.
[49] See further Medcalf 1993.

career, W. H. Auden was clearly interested in both the themes and the metrics of the Horatian ode,[50] while Louis MacNeice produced some interesting translations of individual odes and a poem addressed to the poet, 'Memoranda to Horace' (1962).[51] In the US, Robert Frost as poet of nature has sometimes been aptly compared with Horace, especially in the early 'Hyla Brook' (1916), which seems to echo Horace's poem to the *fons Bandusiae* (*Odes* 3.13).[52] Ezra Pound published at the end of his career a few striking translations from the *Odes*, especially his version of 3.30, while Basil Bunting, an English protégé of Pound, produced some lively versions of Horatian lyric.[53] Other poets from this generation who have produced interesting versions of Horatian odes or other poems are the Americans Robert Lowell and J. V. Cunningham, and the Briton C. H. Sisson, whose modernization of the *Carmen saeculare* is especially notable. For surveys of the landscape see Tomlinson 1993 and Ziolkowski 2005, and the relevant parts of the *Enciclopedia oraziana*.[54]

8. Living Horace

Translations of Horace remain popular in current poetry in English. The US poet and translator David Ferry has produced lively and expansive complete translations of the *Odes* (1997) and of the *Epistles* (2001), while thirty-six poets from either side of the Atlantic collectively translated the *Odes* for McClatchy 2002. The English classical scholar Guy Lee produced a neat verse version of the *Odes* in metres mirroring those of the originals in 1998. Sydenham 2005 and Lyons 2007 give further English versions in a traditional style, while interesting US poetic translations of the complete *Odes* can be found in Krisak 2006 and Kaimowitz 2008, and of the *Satires* in Juster 2008.

Versions of Horatian poems are also widespread. The Northern Irish poet Michael Longley, well known for his brilliant lyric miniaturizations of Homer, has in 'After Horace' and 'The Mad Poet' in *The Ghost Orchid* (1995) juxtaposed witty, brief versions of the beginning and

---

[50] See Talbot 2009.
[51] See Peacock 1992.
[52] See Bacon 2001.
[53] See Pound 1970; Bunting 2000.
[54] Mariotti 1996–8: iii.81–612.

the end of the *Ars poetica* which combine translation with ironic commentary. Seamus Heaney wrote a striking version of *Odes* 1.34 as his response to 9/11, 'Anything Can Happen', adding a pointed reference to the overturning of 'the tallest towers'.[55] In *The Strange Hours Travelers Keep* (2003), the US poet August Kleinzahler presents several pastiche Horatian epistles, including one addressed to Maecenas ('Epistle VIII') which ironically attacks Horace's favoured country life in his own voice. The New Zealander Ian Wedde, in *The Commonplace Odes* (2003), has produced a collection of updated Horatian odes which embed the poet in everyday modern life, while *Rough Translation*, a 2012 collection by another US poet and classical scholar, John Talbot, sets elegant versions of Horatian odes in a New England village. In the UK, the *Epodes*, relatively neglected in Horatian translation generally, have been brilliantly transposed to 1950s working-class steel-town Teesside by Maureen Almond as part of her collection *The Works* (2004), while her *Chasing the Ivy* (2009) sets the first book of *Odes* in the often colourful world of competing modern poets.

[55] In Heaney 2006.

BIBLIOGRAPHY

Ableitinger-Grünberger, D. 1971. *Der junge Horaz und die Politik. Studien zur 7. und 16. Epode.* Heidelberg, Winter.

Allen, W. Jr., Carlson, S. A., Clarke, W. M., Gross, N. P., Hall, R., Hatch, D. F., Kopff, E. C., Payne, M. J., Simms, L. J., and Zartarian, R. C. 1972. 'Horace's First Book of *Epistles* as Letters', *CJ* 69: 119–33.

Almond, M. 2004. *The Works.* Washington, UK, Biscuit.

Almond, M. 2009. *Chasing the Ivy.* Washington, UK, Biscuit.

Altman, J. G. 1982. *Epistolarity.* Columbus, OH, Ohio State University Press.

Ancona, R. 1994. *Time and the Erotic in Horace's Odes*, Durham, NC/London, University of North Carolina Press.

Ancona, R. 2010. 'Female Figures in Horace's *Odes*', in Davis 2010a: 174–92.

Anderson, R. D., Parsons, P. J., and Nisbet, R. G. M. 1979. 'Elegiacs by Gallus from Qaṣr Ibrîm', *JRS* 69: 125–55.

Anderson, W. S. 1982. *Essays on Roman Satire.* Princeton, NJ, Princeton University Press.

Anderson, W. S. (ed.) 1999. *Why Horace?* Wauconda, IL, Bolchazy-Carducci.

Anderson, W. S. 2010. 'Horace's Friendship: Adaptation of a Circular Argument', in Davis 2010a: 34–52.

Armstrong, D. 1989. *Horace.* New Haven, CT, Yale University Press.

Armstrong, D. 2004. 'Horace's *Epistles* 1 and Philodemus', in D. Armstrong, J. Fish, P. A. Johnston, and M. B. Skinner (eds.), *Vergil, Philodemus, and the Augustans.* Austin, TX, University of Texas Press: 267–98.

Armstrong, D. 2010. 'The Biographical and Social Foundations of Horace's Poetic Voice', in Davis 2010a: 7–33.

Asmis, E. A. 1992. 'Neoptolemus and the Classification of Poetry', *CPh* 87: 206–31.

Auhagen, U., Lefèvre, E., and Schäfer, E. (eds.) 2000. *Horaz und Celtis.* Tübingen, Narr.

Babcock, C. L. 1981. '*Carmina operosa*: Critical Approaches to the "Odes" of Horace', *ANRW II.31.3*: 1560–1611.

Bacon, H. 2001. 'Frost and the Ancient Muses', in R. Faggen (ed.), *The Cambridge Companion to Robert Frost.* Cambridge, Cambridge University Press: 75–100.

Baldo, G. 2009. *Eros e storia. Orazio, Carm. I 1–20 e II 1–10.* Verona, Fiorini.

Barchiesi, A. 1996. 'Poetry, Praise and Patronage: Simonides in Book 4 of Horace's *Odes*', *ClAnt* 15: 5–47.

Barchiesi, A. 2000. 'Rituals in Ink: Horace on the Greek Lyric Tradition', in M. Depew and D. Obbink (eds.), *Matrices of Genre. Authors, Canons, and Society.* Cambridge, MA, Harvard University Press: 167–82.

Barchiesi, A. 2001a. 'The Crossing', in Harrison 2001c: 142–73.

Barchiesi, A. 2001b. 'Horace and Iambos: The Poet as Literary Historian', in Cavarzere *et al.* 2001: 141–64.

Barchiesi, A. 2001c. 'Simonides and Horace on the Death of Achilles', in Boedeker and Sider 2001: 255–60.

Barchiesi, A. 2001d. 'Teaching Augustus through Allusion', in A. Barchiesi, *Speaking Volumes*. London, Duckworth: 79–103.

Barchiesi, A. 2002. 'The Uniqueness of the *Carmen saeculare* and its Tradition', in Woodman and Feeney 2002: 107–23.

Becker, C. 1963. *Das Spätwerk des Horaz*. Göttingen, Vandenhoeck & Ruprecht.

Bo, D. 1960. *Q. Horati Flacci Opera III. De Horati Poetico Eloquio*. Turin, Paravia.

Boedeker, D. and Sider, D. (eds.) 2001. *The New Simonides*. New York, Oxford University Press.

Borzák, S. 1984. *Horati Opera*. Leipzig, Teubner.

Bowditch, P. L. 2001. *Horace and the Gift Economy of Patronage*. Berkeley, CA, University of California Press.

Bowditch, P. L. 2010. 'Horace and Imperial Patronage', in Davis 2010a: 55–74.

Bradshaw, A. 1989. 'Horace *in Sabinis*', in C. Deroux (ed.), *Studies in Latin Literature and Roman History V*. Brussels, Latomus: 160–86.

Brink, C. O. 1963. *Horace on Poetry. Prolegomena to the Literary Epistles*. Cambridge, Cambridge University Press.

Brink, C. O. 1971. *Horace on Poetry. The 'Ars Poetica'*. Cambridge, Cambridge University Press.

Brink, C. O. 1982. *Horace on Poetry. Epistles Book II*. Cambridge, Cambridge University Press.

Brown, P. M. 1993. *Horace Satires I*. Warminster, Aris and Phillips.

Büchner, K. 1962. *Horaz*. Wiesbaden, Steiner.

Bunting, B. 2000. *Complete Poems*. Newcastle, Bloodaxe.

Burrow, C. 1993. 'Horace at Home and Abroad: Wyatt and Sixteenth-century Horatianism', in Martindale and Hopkins 1993: 27–49.

Cairns, F. 1972. *Generic Composition in Greek and Roman Poetry*. Edinburgh, Edinburgh University Press.

Cairns, F. 2012. *Roman Lyric. Collected Papers on Catullus and Horace*, Berlin/ Boston, MA, de Gruyter.

Carne-Ross, D. S. and Haynes, K. (eds.) 1996. *Horace in English*. Harmondsworth, Penguin.

Carrubba, R. 1969. *The Epodes of Horace. A Study in Poetic Arrangement*. The Hague, Mouton.

Caston, R. 1997. 'The Fall of the Curtain (Horace S. 2.8)', *TAPhA* 127: 233–56.

Cavarzere, A. 1992. *Orazio. Il libro degli Epodi*. Venice, Marsilio.

Cavarzere, A. 1996. *Sul limitare. Il 'motto' e la poesia di Orazio*. Bologna, Patròn.

Cavarzere, A., Aloni, A., and Barchiesi, A. (eds.) 2001. *Iambic Ideas*. Lanham, MD, Rowman and Littlefield.

Citroni, M. 1995. *Poesia e lettori in Roma antica*. Roma/Bari, Laterza.

Citroni, M. 2001. 'The Memory of Philippi in Horace and the Interpretation of *Epistle* 1.20.23', *CJ* 96: 27–56.

Citroni, M. 2008. 'Horace's *Ars poetica* and the Marvellous', in P. Hardie (ed.), *Paradox and the Marvellous in Augustan Literature and Culture*. Oxford, Oxford University Press: 19–40.

Citti, F. 1994. *Orazio. L'invito a Torquato. Epist. 1, 5*. Bari, Edipuglia.

Collinge, N. R. 1961. *The Structure of Horace's Odes*. London, Oxford University Press.

Commager, H. S. 1957. 'The Function of Wine in Horace's Odes', *TAPhA* 88: 68–80; reprinted in Lowrie 2009a: 33–49.

Commager, H. S. 1962. *The Odes of Horace. A Critical Study*. New Haven, CT, Yale University Press.

Connor, P. J. 1987. *Horace's Lyric Poetry. The Force of Humour*. Berwick, Aureal.

Conte, G. B. 1980. *Il genere e i suoi confini*. Turin, Stampatori.

Conte, G. B. 1986. *The Rhetoric of Imitation*. Ithaca, NY, Cornell University Press.

Costa, C. D. N. (ed.) 1973. *Horace*. London, Routledge.

Courtney, E. 2013a. 'The Transmission of the Text of Horace', in Günther 2013a: 547–60.

Courtney, E. 2013b. 'The Two Books of *Satires*', in Günther 2013a: 63–168.

Cremona, V. 1993. 'Orazio poeta civile', in Ludwig 1993a: 94–123.

Cucchiarelli, A. 2001. *La satira e il poeta. Orazio tra Epodi e Sermones*. Pisa, Giardini.

Cucchiarelli, A. 2010. 'Return to Sender: Horace's *sermo* from the *Epistles* to the *Satires*', in Davis 2010a: 291–318.

Curran, J. V. 1995. *Horace's Epistles, Wieland and the Reader. A Three-way Relationship*. Leeds, W. S. Maney.

Davie, J. N. 2011. *Horace. Satires and Epistles*. Oxford, Oxford University Press.

Davis, G. 1991. *Polyhymnia. The Rhetoric of Horatian Lyric Discourse*. Berkeley, CA, University of California Press.

Davis, G. 2007. 'Wine and the Symposium', in Harrison 2007a: 207–20.

Davis, G. (ed.) 2010a. *A Companion to Horace*. Chichester, Blackwell-Wiley.

Davis, G. 2010b. 'Defining a Lyric Ethos', in Davis 2010a: 105–27.

De Pretis, A. 2002. *'Epistolarity' in the First Book of Horace's Epistles*. Piscataway, NJ, Gorgias.

Delignon, B. 2006. *Les Satires d'Horace et la comédie gréco-latine. Une poétique de l'ambiguïté*. Paris, Peeters.

Delz, J. 1988. Review of Shackleton Bailey 1985, *Gnomon* 60: 495–501.

Dettmer, H. 1983. *Horace: A Study in Structure*. Hildesheim, Olms.

Diederich, S. 1999. *Der Horazkommentar des Porphyrio im Rahmen der kaiserzeitlichen Schul- und Bildungstradition*. Berlin/New York, de Gruyter.

Dilke, O. A. W. 1954. *Horace. Epistles I*. London, Methuen.

Dilke, O. A. W. 1973. 'Horace and the Verse Letter', in Costa 1973: 94–112.

Dilke, O. A. W. 1981. 'The Interpretation of Horace's *Epistles*', *ANRW II.31.3*: 1837–57.

Doblhofer, E. 1966. *Die Augustuspanegyrik des Horaz in formalhistorischer Sicht*. Heidelberg, Winter.

Doblhofer, E. 1981. 'Horaz und Augustus', *ANRW II.31.3*: 1922–86.

Doblhofer, E. 1992. *Horaz in der Forschung nach 1957*. Darmstadt, Wissenschaftliche Buchgesellschaft.

Dunn, F. M., Roberts, D. H., and Fowler, D. P. (eds.) 1997. *Classical Closure*. Princeton, NJ, Princeton University Press.

DuQuesnay, I. M. Le M. 1984. 'Horace and Maecenas: The Propaganda Value of *Sermones* 1', in Woodman and West 1984: 19–58; reprinted in Freudenburg 2009: 42–101.

DuQuesnay, I., M. Le, M. 1995. 'Horace, Odes 4.5: *Pro reditu Imperatoris Caesaris divi filii Augusti*', in Harrison 1995a: 128–87; reprinted in Lowrie 2009a: 271–336.

DuQuesnay, I. M., Le, M. 2002. '*Amicus certus in re incerta cernitur*: Epode 1', in Woodman and Feeney 2002: 17–37.

Eck, W. 2007. *Augustus*. Oxford, Blackwell/Wiley.

Edmunds, L. 1992. *From a Sabine Jar*. Chapel Hill, NC, University of North Carolina Press.

Esser, D. 1976. *Untersuchungen zu den Odenschlüssen bei Horaz*. Meisenheim am Glan, Hain.

Fairclough, H. R. 1927. *Horace. Satires, Epistles and Ars poetica*. London/Cambridge, MA, Heinemann/Harvard University Press.

Fantazzi, C. 2012. *Michael Marullus. Poems*. Cambridge, MA, Harvard University Press.

Fantham, E. 2013a. 'The First Book of Letters', in Günther 2013a: 407–30.

Fantham, E. 2013b. 'The Fourth Book of Odes', in Günther 2013a: 445–66.

Fedeli, P. 1994. *Q. Orazio Flacco. Le satire*. Roma, Libreria dello stato.

Fedeli, P. 1997. *Q. Orazio Flacco. Le epistole*. Roma, Libreria dello stato.

Fedeli, P. and Ciccarelli, I. 2008. *Q. Horati Flacci. Carmina Liber IV*. Florence, Le Monnier.

Feeney, D. 1993. 'Horace and the Greek Lyric Poets', in Rudd 1993a: 41–63; reprinted in Lowrie 2009a: 202–31.

Feeney, D. 1998. *Literature and Religion at Rome*. Cambridge, Cambridge University Press.

Feeney, D. 2002. '*VNA CVM SCRIPTORE MEO*: Poetry, Principate and the Traditions of Literary History in the Epistle to Augustus', in Woodman and Feeney 2002: 172–87; reprinted in Freudenburg 2009: 360–86.

Ferri, R. 1993. *I dispiaceri di un epicureo. Uno studio sulla poetica delle epistole oraziane*. Pisa, Giardini.

Ferri, R. 2007. 'The *Epistles*', in Harrison 2007a: 121–31.

Ferry, D. 1997. *The Odes of Horace*. New York, Farrar, Straus and Giroux.

Ferry, D. 2001. *The Epistles of Horace.* New York, Farrar, Straus and Giroux.

Fiske, G. C. 1920. *Horace and Lucilius.* Madison, WI, University of Wisconsin Press.

Fitzgerald, W. 1988. 'Power and Impotence in Horace's *Epodes*', *Ramus* 17: 176–97.

Flammini, G. 2007–8. 'La strofe alcaica dopo Orazio', *AFLM* 40–41: 39–59.

Ford, P. J. 1997. 'Jean Salmon Macrin's *Epithalamiorum liber* and the Joys of Conjugal Love', in P. J. Ford and I. de Smet (eds.), *Eros et Priapus. Erotisme et obscénité dans la littérature néo-latine.* Geneva, Droz: 64–84.

Fordoński, K. and Urbański, P. 2010. *Casimir Britannicus. English Translations, Paraphrases, and Emulations of the Poetry of Maciej Kazimierz Sarbiewski.* Second edition, London, Modern Humanities Research Association.

Forster, L. 2011. *Selections from Conrad Celtis: 1459–1508.* Cambridge, Cambridge University Press; reprint of 1948 edition.

Fowler, D. P. 1995. 'Horace and the Aesthetics of Politics', in Harrison 1995a: 248–66; reprinted in Lowrie 2009a: 247–70.

Fowler, D. P. 2000. *Roman Constructions. Readings in Postmodern Latin.* Oxford, Oxford University Press.

Fraenkel, E. 1957. *Horace.* Oxford, Oxford University Press.

Francis, P. 1749. *A Poetical Translation of the Works of Horace.* 4 vols, London, Millar.

Freudenburg, K. 1993. *The Walking Muse. Horace on the Theory of Satire.* Princeton, NJ, Princeton University Press.

Freudenburg, K. 1995. 'Canidia at the Feast of Nasidienus (Hor. S. 2.8.95)', *TAPhA* 125: 207–19.

Freudenburg, K. 2001. *Satires of Rome.* Cambridge, Cambridge University Press.

Freudenburg, K. 2002. 'Writing to/through Florus: Criticism and the Addressee in Horace *Epistles* 2.2', *Memoirs of the American Academy in Rome* 47: 33–55; reprinted in Freudenburg 2009: 416–50.

Freudenburg, K. (ed.) 2009. *Horace. Satires and Epistles.* Oxford, Oxford University Press.

Friis-Jensen, K. 1993. 'The Medieval Horace and his Lyrics', in Ludwig 1993a: 257–303.

Friis-Jensen, K. 2007. 'The Reception of Horace in the Middle Ages', in Harrison 2007a: 291–304.

Frischer, B. 1991. *Shifting Paradigms. New Approaches to Horace's Ars Poetica.* Atlanta, GA, Scholars Press.

Frischer, B. 2010. 'The Roman Site Identified as Horace's Villa at Licenza, Italy', in Davis 2010a: 75–90.

Frischer, B., Crawford, J., and De Simone, M. 2006. *The Horace's Villa Project, 1997–2003.* 2 vols, Oxford, Archaeopress.

Gaisser, J. H. 1994. 'The Roman Odes at School', *CW* 87: 443–56.

Gaskin, R. 2013. *Horace and Housman. Parallels.* New York, Palgrave Macmillan.

Ghiselli, A. 1974. *Orazio, Ode 1,1. Saggio di analisi formale*. Bologna, Patròn; second edition 1983.

Gillespie, S. 1993. 'Horace's *Ode* 3.29: Dryden's "Masterpiece in English"', in Martindale and Hopkins 1993: 148–58.

Gladstone, W. E. 1894. *The Odes of Horace*. London, John Murray.

Glomski, J. 1987. 'The Role of *imitatio* in J. Kochanowski's *Elegiae. Lyricorum libellus* and *Pieśni*', in *Oxford Slavonic Papers* n.s. 20: 34–59.

Goad, C. 1918. *Horace in the English Literature of the Eighteenth Century*. New Haven, CT, Yale University Press; reprinted New York, Haskell House Publishers, 1967.

Gold, B. K. 1992. 'Openings in Horace's *Satires* and *Odes*: Poet, Patron, and Audience', *YClS* 29:161–85.

Gowers, E. 1993a. 'Horace *Satires* I. 5: An Inconsequential Journey', *PCPhS* 39: 48–66; reprinted in Freudenburg 2009: 156–81.

Gowers, E. 1993b. *The Loaded Table*. Oxford, Oxford University Press.

Gowers, E. 2002. 'Blind Eyes and Cut Throats: Amnesia and Silence in Horace *Satires* 1.7', *CPh* 97: 145–61.

Gowers, E. 2003. 'Fragments of Autobiography in Horace *Satires* I', *ClAnt* 22: 55–91.

Gowers, E. 2009. 'The Ends of the Beginning: Horace, *Satires* I', in Houghton and Wyke 2009: 39–60.

Gowers, E. 2012. *Horace, Satires I*. Cambridge, Cambridge University Press.

Grassmann, V. 1966. *Die erotischen Epoden des Horaz*. Munich, Beck.

Green, R. P. H. 2000. 'Davidic Psalm and Horatian Ode: Five Poems of George Buchanan', *Renaissance Studies* 14: 91–111.

Green, R. P. H. 2009. 'The Heavens are Telling: A Psalm-paraphrase-poem Analysed', in P. J. Ford and R. P. H. Green (eds.), *George Buchanan. Poet and Dramatist*. Swansea, Classical Press of Wales: 75–94.

Green, R. P. H. 2011. *George Buchanan. Poetic Paraphrase of the Psalms of David*. Geneva, Droz.

Griffin, J. 1985. *Latin Poets and Roman Life*. London, Duckworth.

Griffin, J. 1993. 'Horace in the Thirties', in Rudd 1993a: 1–22.

Griffin, J. 2002. 'Look Your Last on Lyric: Horace *Odes* 4.15', in T. P. Wiseman (ed.), *Classics in Progress*. Oxford, Oxford University Press: 311–32.

Griffiths, A. 2002. 'The *Odes*: Just Where Do You Draw the Line?', in Woodman and Feeney 2002: 65–79.

Grimal, P. 1958. *Horace*. Paris, Seuil.

Gruber, J. 1997. 'Horaz im deutschen Renaissancehumanismus', *Gymnasium* 104: 227–44.

Günther, H-G. (ed.) 2013a. *Brill's Companion to Horace*. Leiden, Brill.

Günther, H-G. 2013b. 'The *Carmen saeculare*', in Günther 2013a: 431–44.

Günther, H-G. 2013c. 'The Second Book of Letters', in Günther 2013a: 467–98.

Habinek, T. 2005. *The World of Roman Song*. Baltimore, MD, Johns Hopkins University Press.

Hamilton, J. T. 2001. 'Thunder from a Clear Sky: On Lessing's Redemption of Horace', *Modern Language Quarterly* 62: 203–18.

Hardie, P. 1997. 'Fifth-century Athenian and Augustan Images of the Barbarian Other', *Classics Ireland* 4: 46–56.

Hardie, P. and Moore, H. (eds.) 2010. *Classical Literary Careers and Their Reception*. Cambridge, Cambridge University Press.

Hardwick, L. 2003. *Reception Studies*. Greece & Rome New Surveys in the Classics 33. Oxford, Oxford University Press.

Hardwick, L. and Stray, C. (eds.) 2008. *A Companion to Classical Receptions*. Oxford, Blackwell.

Harrison, S. J. 1988. 'Deflating the *Odes*: Horace, *Epistles* 1.20', *CQ* 38: 473–6.

Harrison, S. J. 1990. 'The Praise Singer: Horace, Censorinus and *Odes* 4.8', *JRS* 80: 31–43.

Harrison, S. J. (ed.) 1995a. *Homage to Horace. A Bimillenary Celebration*. Oxford, Oxford University Press.

Harrison, S. J. 1995b. 'Horace, Pindar, Iullus Antonius, and Augustus: *Odes* 4. 2', in Harrison 1995a: 108–27.

Harrison, S. J. 1995c. 'Poetry, Philosophy, and Letter-writing in Horace *Epistles* 1', in D. Innes, H. Hine, and C. Pelling (eds.), *Ethics and Rhetoric: Classical Essays for Donald Russell on His Seventy-fifth Birthday*. Oxford, Oxford University Press: 47–61; reprinted in Freudenburg 2009: 270–87.

Harrison, S. J. 1997. 'Archpoet, Poem IV and Some Horatian Intertexts', *MLatJB* 32: 37–42.

Harrison, S. J. 2001a. 'Horace and Simonides', in Boedeker and Sider 2001: 261–71.

Harrison, S. J. 2001b. 'Some Generic Problems in Horace's *Epodes*: Or, on (Not) Being Archilochus', in Cavarzere *et al.* 2001: 165–86.

Harrison, S. J. (ed.) 2001c. *Texts, Ideas, and the Classics. Scholarship, Theory, and Classical Literature*. Oxford, Oxford University Press.

Harrison, S. J. 2002. Review of Schmidt 2002b, *Bryn Mawr Classical Review* 2002.11.10.

Harrison, S. J. 2003. Review of McClatchy 2002, *Bryn Mawr Classical Review* 2003.03.05.

Harrison, S. J. 2004. 'Lyric Middles: The Turn at the Centre in Horace's *Odes*', in Kyriakidis and Di Martino 2004: 81–102.

Harrison, S. J. (ed.) 2007a. *The Cambridge Companion to Horace*. Cambridge, Cambridge University Press.

Harrison, S. J. 2007b. *Generic Enrichment in Vergil and Horace*. Oxford, Oxford University Press.

Harrison, S. J. 2007c. 'Horace and the Construction of the Victorian Gentleman', *Helios* 33: 207–22.

Harrison, S. J. 2007d. 'Horatian Self-representations', in Harrison 2007a: 22–35.

Harrison, S. J. 2008. 'Horace *Epistles* 2: The Last Horatian Book of *Sermones?*', *PLLS* 13: 173–86.

Harrison, S. J. 2010. 'There and Back Again: Horace's Literary Career', in Hardie and Moore 2010: 39–58.

Harrison, S. J. 2012. 'George Buchanan: The Scottish Horace', in L. B. T. Houghton and G. Manuwald (eds.), *Neo-Latin Poetry in the British Isles*. London, Bristol Classical Press: 155–72.

Harrison, S. J. 2013a. 'Author and Speaker(s) in Horace *Satires* 2', in A. Marmodoro and J. Hill (eds.), *The Author's Voice in Classical and Late Antiquity*. Oxford, Oxford University Press: 153–74.

Harrison, S. J. 2013b. 'Didactic and Lyric in Horace *Odes* 2: Lucretius and Vergil', in T. D. Papanghelis, S. J. Harrison, and S. A. Frangoulidis (eds.), *Generic Interfaces in Latin Literature. Encounters, Interactions and Transformations*. Berlin, de Gruyter: 367–84.

Heaney, S. 2006. *District and Circle*. London, Faber.

Heinze, R. 1923. 'Die Horazische Ode', *Neue Jahrbücher für das klassische Altertum* 51: 153–68; reprinted in R. Heinze *Vom Geist des Römertums*. Leipzig, Teubner: 185–212; English translation in Lowrie 2009a: 11–32.

Henderson, J. 1998. *Writing Down Rome*. Oxford, Oxford University Press.

Henderson, J. 1999. *Fighting for Rome*. Cambridge, Cambridge University Press.

Heyworth, S. J. 1993. 'Horace's *Ibis*: On the Titles, Unity, and Contents of the *Epodes*', *PLLS* 7: 85–96.

Heyworth, S. J. 2001. 'Catullan Iambics, Catullan *Iambi*', in Cavarzere *et al.* 2001: 117–40.

Hills, P. D. 2005. *Horace*. London, Bristol Classical Press.

Holder, A. 1894. *Pomponi Porfyrionis Commentum in Horatium Flaccum*. Innsbruck, Wagner.

Holzberg, N. 2007. *Horaz. Eine Bibliographie*. Munich, privately printed; available online at http://www.niklasholzberg.com/Homepage/Bibliographien.html.

Holzberg, N. 2008. 'A Sensitive, Even Weak and Feeble Disposition? C. Valgius Rufus and His Elegiac Ego', in A. Arweiler and M. Möller (eds.), *Vom Selbst-Verständnis in Antike und Neuzeit / Notions of the Self in Antiquity and Beyond*. Berlin/New York, de Gruyter: 21–32.

Holzberg, N. 2009. *Horaz*. Munich, Beck.

Hooley, D. 2012. 'Roman Satire and Epigram', in Hopkins and Martindale 2012: 217–54.

Hopkins, D. 1993. 'Cowley's Horatian Mice', in Martindale and Hopkins 1993: 103–26.

Hopkins, D. and Martindale, C. (eds.) 2012. *The Oxford History of Classical Reception. Volume 3: 1660–1790*. Oxford, Oxford University Press.

Horsfall, N. M. 1993. *La villa Sabina di Orazio. Il galateo della gratitudine*. Venosa, Osanna.

Horsfall, N. M. 1998. 'The First Person Singular in Horace's *Carmina*', in P. E. Knox and C. Foss (eds.), *Style and Tradition. Studies in Honor of Wendell Clausen*. Stuttgart, Teubner: 40–54.

Houghton, L. B. T. 2009. 'Two Letters to Horace: Petrarch and Andrew Lang', in Houghton and Wyke 2009: 161–81.

Houghton, L. B. T. and Wyke, M. (eds.) 2009. *Perceptions of Horace*. Cambridge, Cambridge University Press.

Hubbard, M. 1973. 'The *Odes*', in Costa 1973: 1–28.

Hutchinson, G. O. 2007. 'Horace and Archaic Greek Poetry', in Harrison 2007a: 36–49.

Hutchinson, G. O. 2008. *Talking Books*. Oxford, Oxford University Press.

Ingleheart, J. 2010. *Ovid Tristia 2*. Oxford, Oxford University Press.

Janko, R. 2000. *Philodemus, On Poems. Book One*. Oxford, Oxford University Press.

Jocelyn, H. D. 2004. 'Brink, Charles Oscar (1907–1994)', *Oxford Dictionary of National Biography*. Oxford, Oxford University Press; online at http://www.oxforddnb.com/.

Johnson, T. 2004. *A Symposion of Praise*. Madison, WI, University of Wisconsin Press.

Johnson, T. *Horace's Iambic Criticism. Casting Blame*. Leiden, Brill.

Johnson, W. R. 1993. *Horace and the Dialectic of Freedom*. Ithaca, NY, Cornell University Press.

Johnson, W. R. 2010. 'The *Epistles*', in Davis 2010a: 319–33.

Juster, A. M. 2008. *The Satires of Horace*. Philadelphia, PA, University of Pennsylvania Press.

Kaimowitz, J. 2008. *The Odes of Horace*. Baltimore, MD, Johns Hopkins University Press.

Kalinina, A. 2007. *Der Horazkommentar des Pomponius Porphyrio. Untersuchungen zu seiner Terminologie und Textgeschichte*. Stuttgart, Steiner.

Keller, O. 1902. *Pseudacronis scholia in Horatium vetustiora*. Leipzig, Teubner.

Keller, O. and Holder, A. 1899. *Q. Horati Flacci Opera*. 2 vols, Leipzig, Teubner.

Keller, O. and Holder, A. 1925. *Q. Horati Flacci Opera*. Second edition, Leipzig, Teubner.

Kiessling, A. 1884. *Q. Horatius Flaccus. Oden und Epoden*. Berlin, Weidmann.

Kiessling, A. 1886. *Q. Horatius Flaccus. Satiren*. Berlin, Weidmann.

Kiessling, A. 1889. *Q. Horatius Flaccus. Briefe*. Berlin, Weidmann.

Kiessling, A. and Heinze, R. 1930. *Q. Horatius Flaccus. Oden und Epoden*. Seventh edition, Berlin, Weidmann.

Kiessling, A. and Heinze, R. 1960. *Q. Horatius Flaccus. Oden und Epoden*. Tenth edition, Berlin, Weidmann.

Kilpatrick, R. S. 1986. *The Poetry of Friendship. Horace, Epistles I*. Edmonton, University of Alberta Press.

Kilpatrick, R. S. 1990. *The Poetry of Criticism. Horace Epistles II and Ars Poetica.* Edmonton, University of Alberta Press.

Kissel, W. 1981. 'Horaz 1936–1975', *ANRW II.31.3*: 1403–1558.

Kissel, W. 1994. 'Horazbibliographie 1976–91', in S. Koster (ed.), *Horaz-Studien.* Erlangen, Universitäts-Bibliothek: 115–92.

Kleinzahler, A. 2003. *The Strange Hours Travelers Keep.* New York, Farrar Straus & Giroux.

Klingner, F. 1953. *Römische Geisteswelt.* Wiesbaden, Dieterich.

Klingner, F. 1959. *Horatius. Opera.* Third edition, Leipzig, Teubner.

Klingner, F. 1964. *Studien zur griechischen und römischen Literatur.* Zürich, Artemis.

Knight, S. and Tilg, S. (eds.) 2014. *The Oxford Handbook of Neo-Latin.* Oxford, Oxford University Press.

Knorr, O. 2004. *Verborgene Kunst. Argumentationsstruktur und Buchaufbau in den Satiren des Horaz.* Hildesheim, Olms.

Knox, P. E. 2013. 'Language, Style and Metre in Horace', in Günther 2013a: 527–546.

Krasser, H. 1995. *Horazische Denkfiguren.* Göttingen, Vandenhoeck & Ruprecht.

Krasser, H. and Schmidt, E. A. (eds.) 1996. *Zeitgenosse Horaz. Der Dichter und seine Leser seit zwei Jahrtausenden.* Tübingen, Narr.

Krisak, L. 2006. *The Odes of Horace.* Manchester, Carcanet.

Kroll, W. 1924. *Studien zum Verständnis der römischen Literatur.* Stuttgart, Metzler.

Kyriakidis, S. and De Martino, F. (eds.) 2004. *Middles in Latin Poetry.* Bari, Levante.

Labate, M. 1981. *Orazio. Satire.* Milan, Rizzoli.

La Penna, A. 1963. *Orazio e l' ideologia del principato.* Turin, Einaudi.

La Penna, A. 1969. *Orazio e la morale mondana europea.* Florence, Sansoni.

La Penna, A. 1993. *Saggi e studi su Orazio.* Florence, Sansoni.

Laird, A. 2007. 'The *Ars poetica*', in Harrison 2007a: 132–43.

Lee, Guy (1998). *The Odes of Horace.* Leeds, Cairns.

Lefèvre, E. 1993. 'Waren horazische Gedichte zum "öffentlichen" Vortrag bestimmt?', in G. Vogt-Spira (ed.), *Beiträge zur mündlichen Kultur der Römer.* Tübingen, Narr: 143–57.

Lefèvre, E. and Schäfer, E. (eds.) 2008. *Michael Marullus. Ein Grieche als Renaissancedichter in Italien.* Tübingen, Narr.

Lefèvre, E. and Schäfer, E. 2010. *Beiträge zu den Sylvae des neulateinischen Barockdichters Jakob Balde.* Tübingen, Narr.

Lefkowitz, M. 1991. *First-person Fictions. Pindar's Poetic 'I'.* Oxford, Oxford University Press.

Lejay, E. 1911. *Horace. Satires.* Paris, Hachette.

Levi, P. 1997. *Horace. A Life.* London, Duckworth.

Longley, M. 1995. *The Ghost Orchid.* London, Cape.

Longobardi, C. 2010. 'Strofe saffica e innologia: l'apprendimento dei metri nella scuola Cristiana', *Paideia* 65: 371–80.

Lowrie, M. 1995. 'A Parade of Lyric Predecessors: Horace *C.* 1.12–1.18', *Phoenix* 49: 33–48; reprinted in Lowrie 2009a: 337–55.

Lowrie, M. 1997. *Horace's Narrative Odes*. Oxford, Oxford University Press.

Lowrie, M. (ed.) 2009a. *Horace. Odes and Epodes*. Oxford, Oxford University Press.

Lowrie, M. 2009b. *Writing, Performance, and Authority in Augustan Rome*. Oxford, Oxford University Press.

Ludwig, W. (ed.) 1993a. *Horace. L'oeuvre et les imitations. Un siècle d'interprétation*. Geneva, Fondation Hardt.

Ludwig, W. 1993b. 'Horazrezeption in der Renaissance oder die Renaissance des Horaz', in Ludwig 1993a: 305–71.

Lumsden, A. 1947. *Garcilaso de la Vega as a Latin Poet*. Cambridge, Cambridge University Press.

Lyne, R. O. A. M. 1980. *The Latin Love Poets*. Oxford, Oxford University Press.

Lyne, R. O. A. M. 1995. *Horace. Behind the Public Poetry*. New Haven, CT, Yale University Press.

Lyons, S. 2007. *Horace's Odes and the Mystery of Do-Re-Mi*. Oxford, Oxbow.

Macleod, C. 1979. 'The Poetry of Ethics: Horace, *Epistles* I', *JRS* 69: 16–27; reprinted in C. Macleod, *Collected Essays*. Oxford, Oxford University Press, 1983: 280–91, and in Freudenburg 2009: 245–69.

Malcovati, E. 1977. 'Augusto fonte di Suetonio', in W. Kraus, A. Primmer, and H. Schwalb (eds.), *Festschrift für Rudolf Hanslik zum 70. Geburstag*. Vienna, Böhlau: 187–95.

Mankin, D. 1995. *Horace. Epodes*. Cambridge, Cambridge University Press.

Marchesi, I. 2005. 'In Memory of Simonides: Poetry and Mnemotechnics chez Nasidienus', *TAPhA* 135: 393–402.

Mariotti, S. (ed.) 1996-8. *Orazio. Enciclopedia oraziana*. 3 vols, Rome, Treccani.

Martin, T. 1860. *The Odes of Horace*. London, J. W. Parker.

Martin, T. 1881. *The Works of Horace*. Edinburgh: Blackwood.

Martindale, C. and Hopkins, D. (eds.) 1993. *Horace Made New*. Cambridge, Cambridge University Press.

Martindale, C. and Thomas, R. (eds.) 2006. *Classics and the Uses of Reception*. Oxford, Blackwell.

Maurach, G. 1968. 'Der Grundriß von Horazens erstem Epistelbuch', *AClass* 11: 73–124.

Mayer, R. 1985. 'Horace on Good Manners', *PCPhS* 31: 33–46.

Mayer, R. 1986. 'Horace's *Epistles* I and Philosophy', *AJPh* 107: 55–73.

Mayer, R. 1994. *Horace. Epistles Book I*. Cambridge, Cambridge University Press.

Mayer, R. 1995. 'Horace's *moyen de parvenir*', in Harrison 1995a: 279–95.

Mayer, R. 2003. 'Persona(l) Problems: The Literary Persona in Antiquity Revisited', *MD* 50: 55–80.

Mayer, R. 2012. *Horace. Odes Book I*. Cambridge, Cambridge University Press.

McClatchy, J. D. (ed.) 2002. *Horace. The Odes. New Translations by Contemporary Poets*. Princeton, NJ, Princeton University Press.

McFarlane, I. D. 1981. *Buchanan*. London, Faber.

McGann, M. J. 1969. *Studies in Horace's First Book of Epistles*. Brussels, Latomus.

McGann, M. J. 2007. 'The Reception of Horace in the Renaissance', in Harrison 2007a: 305–17.

McGinn, T. 2001. 'Satire and the Law: The Case of Horace', *PCPhS* 47: 81–102.

McNeill, R. L. B. 2001. *Horace. Image, Identity, and Audience*. Baltimore, MD, Johns Hopkins University Press.

McNeill, R. L. B. 2009. 'Horace', in *Oxford Bibliographies*, http://www.oxfordbibliographies.com/.

Medcalf, S. 1993. 'Kipling's Horace', in Martindale and Hopkins 1993: 217–39.

Mette, H. J. 1961. 'Genus tenue und *mensa tenuis* bei Horaz', *MH* 18: 136–9; English version in Lowrie 2009a: 50–55.

Minadeo, R. 1982. *The Golden Plectrum. Sexual Symbolism in Horace's Odes*. Amsterdam, Rodopi.

Minarini, A. 1989. *Lucidus ordo. L'architettura della lirica oraziana (libri I–III)*. Bologna, Patròn.

Mindt, N. 2007. *Die meta-sympotischen Oden und Epoden des Horaz*. Göttingen, Edition Ruprecht.

Moles, J. L. 2002. 'Poetry, Philosophy, Politics, and Play: *Epistles* I', in Woodman and Feeney 2002: 141–57; reprinted in Freudenburg 2009: 308–33.

Moles, J. L. 2007. 'Philosophy and Ethics', in Harrison 2007a: 165–80.

Mondin, L. 1997. *L'Ode I,4 di Orazio tra modelli e struttura*. Naples, Loffredo.

Money, D. K. 1998. *The English Horace. Anthony Alsop and the Tradition of British Latin Verse*. Oxford, Oxford University Press.

Money, D. K. 2007. 'The Reception of Horace in the Seventeenth and Eighteenth Centuries', in Harrison 2007a: 318–33.

Morello, R. and Morrison, A. D. (eds.) 2007. *Ancient Letters*. Oxford, Oxford University Press.

Morgan, L. 2010. *Musa Pedestris. Metre and Meaning in Roman Verse*. Oxford, Oxford University Press.

Moritz, L. A. 1968. 'Some "Central" Thoughts on Horace's *Odes*', *CQ* 18: 116–31.

Morrison, A. D. 2007. 'Didacticism and Epistolarity in Horace, *Epistles* 1', in Morello and Morrison 2007: 107–32.

Moul, V. 2010. *Jonson, Horace and the Classical Tradition*. Cambridge, Cambridge University Press.

Muecke, F. 1993. *Horace. Satires II*. Warminster, Aris and Phillips.

Muecke, F. 1995. 'Law, Rhetoric, and Genre in Horace, *Satires* 2.1', in Harrison 1995a: 203–18.

Muecke, F. 1997. 'Lingua e stile', in Mariotti 1996–8: ii.755–87.

Muecke, F. 2007. 'The *Satires*', in Harrison 2007a: 105–20.

Munk Olsen, B. 1996. 'The Production of the Classics in the Eleventh and Twelfth Centuries', in C. A. Chavannes-Mazel, and M. M. Smith (eds.), *Medieval Manuscripts of the Latin Classics. Production and Use.* Los Altos Hills, CA, Anderson Lovelance: 1–17.

Murray, O. 1985. 'Symposium and Genre in the Poetry of Horace', *JRS* 75: 39–50; reprinted in Rudd 1993a: 89–105.

Murray, O. (ed.) 1990. *Sympotica*. Oxford, Oxford University Press.

Nadeau, Y. 2008. *Erotica for Caesar Augustus. A Study of the Love-poetry of Horace, Carmina, Books I to III*. Brussels, Latomus.

Newman, J. K. 2011. *Horace as Outsider*. Hildesheim, Olms.

Nisbet, R. G. M. 1959. 'Notes on Horace *Epistles* 1', *CQ* 9: 73–6; reprinted in Nisbet 1995: 1–5.

Nisbet, R. G. M. 1962. '*Romanae fidicen lyrae*: The *Odes* of Horace', in J. P. Sullivan (ed.), *Critical Essays on Roman Literature. Elegy and Lyric*. London, Routledge: 181–218.

Nisbet, R. G. M. 1984. 'Horace's *Epodes* and History', in Woodman and West 1984: 1–18; reprinted in Nisbet 1995: 161–81.

Nisbet, R. G. M. 1986. 'A Rival Teubner Horace', *CR* n.s. 36: 227–34; reprinted in Nisbet 1995: 192–201.

Nisbet, R. G. M. 1995. *Collected Papers on Latin Literature*. Oxford, Oxford University Press.

Nisbet, R. G. M. 1999. 'The Word Order of Horace's *Odes*', in J. N. Adams and R. G. Mayer (eds.), *Aspects of the Language of Latin Poetry*. Oxford, Oxford University Press: 135–54.

Nisbet, R. G. M. 2007. 'Horace: Life and Chronology', in Harrison 2007a: 7–21.

Nisbet, R. G. M. and Hubbard, M. 1970. *A Commentary on Horace. Odes I*. Oxford, Oxford University Press.

Nisbet, R. G. M. and Hubbard, M. 1978. *A Commentary on Horace. Odes II*. Oxford, Oxford University Press.

Nisbet, R. G. M. and Rudd, N. 2004. *A Commentary on Horace. Odes III*. Oxford, Oxford University Press.

Nock, A. D. 1933. *Conversion*. Oxford, Oxford University Press.

Noske, G. 1969. *Quaestiones Pseudoacroneae*. Dissertation, Munich.

Nuttall, A. D. 1993. 'Marvell and Horace: Colour and Translucency', in Martindale and Hopkins 1993: 86–102.

Oliensis, E. 1991. 'Canidia, Canicula, and the Decorum of Horace's *Epodes*', *Arethusa* 24: 107–38; reprinted in Lowrie 2009a: 160–87.

Oliensis, E. 1998. *Horace and the Rhetoric of Authority*. Cambridge, Cambridge University Press.

Oliensis, E. 2007. 'Erotics and Gender', in Harrison 2007a: 221–34.

Orlando, S. 1993. *Pietro Metastasio. Dell'arte poetica. Epistola di Q. Orazio Flacco a' Pisoni*. Florence, Polistampa.

Page, T. E. 1886. *Horace. Odes and Epodes*. London, Macmillan.

Palmer, A.-M. 1989. *Prudentius on the Martyrs*. Oxford, Oxford University Press.

Paschalis, M. (ed.) 2002. *Horace and Greek Lyric Poetry*. Rethymnon, Department of Philology, University of Crete.

Pasquali, G. 1920. *Orazio Lirico*. Florence, Le Monnier.

Peacock, A. J. 1992. 'Louis MacNeice: Transmitting Horace', *Revista Alicantina de Estudios Ingleses* 5: 119–30.

Pearce, T. E. V. 1966. 'The Enclosing Word Order in the Latin Hexameter', *CQ* 16: 140–71, 298–320.

Pelling, C. B. R. 1996. 'The Triumviral Period', in A. K. Bowman, E. Champlin, and A. W. Lintott (eds.), *The Cambridge Ancient History. Vol. 10. The Augustan Empire, 43 BC–AD 69*. Cambridge, Cambridge University Press: 1–69.

Perret, J. 1959. *Horace*. Paris, Hatier.

Perret, J. 1964. *Horace*. New York, New York University Press.

Pöschl, V. 1956. *Horaz und die Politik*. Heidelberg, Winter.

Pöschl, V. 1970. *Horazische Lyrik. Interpretationen*. Heidelberg, Winter.

Porter, D. H. 1987. *Horace's Poetic Journey*. Princeton, NJ, Princeton University Press.

Porter, J. I. 1995. 'Content and Form in Philodemus: The History of an Evasion', in D. Obbink (ed.), *Philodemus on Poetry*. New York, Oxford University Press: 97–147.

Pound, E. 1970. *The Translations of Ezra Pound*. London, Faber.

Pucci, J. 1991. 'Prudentius' Readings of Horace in the *Cathemerinon*', *Latomus* 50: 677–90.

Putnam, M. C. J. 1986. *Artifices of Eternity. Horace's Fourth Book of Odes*. Ithaca, NY, Cornell University Press.

Putnam, M. C. J. 2000. *Horace's Carmen saeculare*. New Haven, CT, Yale University Press.

Putnam, M. C. J. 2006. *Poetic Interplay. Catullus and Horace*. Princeton, NJ, Princeton University Press.

Putnam, M. C. J. 2009. *Sannazaro. Latin Poetry*. Cambridge, MA, Harvard University Press.

Quinn, K. 1963. *Latin Explorations*. London, Routledge.

Quinn, K. 1980. *Horace. Odes*. London, Macmillan.

Quint, M.-B. 1988. *Untersuchungen zur mittelalterlichen Horaz-Rezeption*. Frankfurt am Main, Lang.

Race, W. H. 2010. 'Horace's Debt to Pindar', in Davis 2010a: 147–73.

Reinhardt, T. 2013. 'The *Ars poetica*', in Günther 2013a: 499–526.

Richlin, A. 1991. 'Introduction', in A. Richlin (ed.), *Pornography and Representation in Greece and Rome*. Oxford, Oxford University Press: xi–xxiii.

Richlin, A. 1992. *The Garden of Priapus*. Second edition, Oxford, Oxford University Press.

Robin, D. 2009. *Francesco Filelfo. Odes*. Cambridge, MA, Harvard University Press.

Rolfe, J. C. 1914. *Suetonius II*. Cambridge, MA/London, Harvard University Press/Heinemann.

Rossi, L. E. 1998. 'Orazio, un lirico greco senza musica', *Seminari Romani di Cultura Greca* 1: 163–81; English version in Lowrie 2009a: 356–77.

Rudd, N. 1966. *The Satires of Horace*. Cambridge, Cambridge University Press.

Rudd, N. 1976. *Lines of Enquiry*. Cambridge, Cambridge University Press.

Rudd, N. 1987. *Horace. Satires and Epistles; Persius. Satires*. Harmondsworth, Penguin.

Rudd, N. 1989. *Horace. Epistles Book II and Epistle to the Pisones ('Ars poetica')*. Cambridge, Cambridge University Press.

Rudd, N. (ed.) 1993a. *Horace 2000. A Celebration. Essays for the Bimillennium*. London, Bristol Classical Press.

Rudd, N. 1994. *The Classical Tradition in Operation*. Toronto, University of Toronto Press.

Rudd, N. 2004. *Horace. Odes and Epodes*. Cambridge, MA, Harvard University Press.

Rudd, N. 2005. *The Common Spring. Essays on Latin and English Poetry*. Bristol, Bristol Phoenix Press.

Rudd, N. 2007. Review of Harrison 2007a, *Bryn Mawr Classical Review* 2007.05.25.

Russell, D. A. 1973. '*Ars poetica*', in Costa 1973: 113–34; reprinted in A. Laird (ed.), *Ancient Literary Criticism*. Oxford, Oxford University Press, 2005: 325–46.

Santirocco, M. 1986. *Unity and Design in Horace's Odes*. Chapel Hill, NC, University of North Carolina Press.

Santirocco, M. (ed.) 1994. *Recovering Horace*. = *Classical World* 87.5. Baltimore, MD, Johns Hopkins University Press.

Schäfer, E. 1976. *Deutscher Horaz. Conrad Celtis. Georg Fabricius. Paul Melissus. Jacob Balde. Die Nachwirking des Horaz in der neulateinischen Dichtung Deutschlands*. Wiesbaden, Steiner.

Schäfer, E. (ed.) 2004. *Johannes Secundus und die Römische Liebeselegie*. Tübingen, Narr.

Schäfer, E. 2008. *Conrad Celtis. Oden/Epoden/Jahrhundertlied. Libri odarum quattuor, cum epodo et saeculari carmine*. Tübingen, Narr.

Schäfer, E. (ed.) 2006. *Sarbiewski. Der polnische Horaz*. Tübingen, Narr.

Schlegel, C. 2005. *Satire and the Threat of Speech. Horace's Satires Book 1*. Madison, WI, University of Wisconsin Press.

Schmidt, E. A. 1977. '*Amica vis pastoribus*: der Jambiker Horaz in seinem Epodenbuch', *Gymnasium* 84: 401–23.

Schmidt, E. A. 2002a. 'Horaz und die Erneuerung der deutschen Lyrik im 18. Jahrhundert', in Schmidt 2002b: 380–428.

Schmidt, E. A. 2002b. *Zeit und Form. Dichtungen des Horaz*. Heidelberg, Winter.

Schmidt, E. A. 2003–4. '"Auf den Flügeln des Choriambs": Herder und Horaz', *IJCT* 10: 416–37.

Schmitz, T. 1994. 'L'ode latine pendant la renaissance française: un catalogue des odes publiées au seizième siècle', *Humanistica Lovaniensia* 43: 173–219.

Schnegg-Köhler, B. 2002. *Die augusteischen Säkularspiele*, Munich, Saur.

Schrijvers, P. H. 1973. 'Comment terminer une ode?', *Mnemosyne* 26: 140–59.

Scodel, J. 2010. 'Lyric', in G. Braden, R. Cummings, and S. Gillespie (eds.), *The Oxford History of Literary Translation in English. Volume 2. 1550–1660*. Oxford, Oxford University Press: 212–47.

Scodel, R. 1987. 'Horace, Lucilius, and Callimachean Polemic', *HSPh* 91: 199–215; reprinted in Freudenburg 2009: 212–30.

Seager, R. 1993. 'Horace and Augustus: Poetry and Policy', in Rudd 1993a: 23–40.

Shackleton Bailey, D. R. 1982. *Profile of Horace*. London, Duckworth.

Shackleton Bailey, D. R. 1985. *Horatius. Opera*. Stuttgart, Teubner.

Sharland, S. 2010. *Horace in Dialogue. Bakhtinian Readings in the Satires*, Oxford, Lang.

Sharland, S. 2011. 'Ghostly Guests and Venomous Snakes: Traces of Civil War in Horace, *Satires* 2.8', *AClass* 54: 79–100.

Showerman, G. 1922. *Horace and His Influence*. London, Harrap.

Slings, S. R. (ed.) 1990. *The Poet's 'I' in Archaic Greek Lyric*. Amsterdam, VU University Press.

Soubeille, G. 1998. *Jean Salmon Macrin. Épithalames et odes*. Paris, Champion.

Sowerby, R. 2012. 'Horatianism', in Hopkins and Martindale 2012: 255–86.

Stack, F. 1985. *Pope and Horace. Studies in Imitation*. Cambridge, Cambridge University Press.

Stemplinger, E. 1906. *Das Fortleben der horazischen Lyrik seit der Renaissance*. Leipzig, Teubner.

Stemplinger, E. 1921. *Horaz im Urteil der Jahrhunderte*. Leipzig, Dieterich.

Stevenson, J. 2009. 'Horace and Learned Ladies', in Houghton and Wyke 2009: 182–99.

Strauss Clay, J. 2010. 'Horace and Lesbian Lyric', in Davis 2010a: 128–46.

Sutherland, E. H. 2002. *Horace's Well-trained Reader*. Frankfurt am Main, Lang.

Sydenham, C. 2005. *Horace. The Odes*. London, Duckworth.

Syme, R. 1939. *The Roman Revolution*. Oxford, Oxford University Press.

Syme, R. 1986. *The Augustan Aristocracy*. Oxford, Oxford University Press.

Syndikus, H. P. 1972–3. *Die Lyrik des Horaz. 2 vols, Darmstadt, Wissenschaftliche Buchgesellschaft; third edition 2001*.

Syndikus, H. P. 1995. 'Some Structures in Horace's *Odes*', in Harrison 1995a: 17–31.

Talbot, J. 2009. 'A Late Flowering of English Alcaics', in Houghton and Wyke 2009: 305–23.

Talbot, J. 2012. *Rough Translation*. Cincinnati, OH, David Robert.

Tarrant, R. J. 1983. 'Horace', in L. D. Reynolds (ed.), *Texts and Transmission. A Survey of the Latin Classics*. Oxford, Oxford University Press: 182–6.

Tarrant, R. J. 1995. '*Da Capo* Structure in Some *Odes* of Horace', in Harrison 1995a: 32–49.

Tarrant, R. J. 2007. 'Ancient Receptions of Horace', in Harrison 2007a: 277–90.

Thayer, M. R. 1916. *The Influence of Horace on the English Poets of the Nineteenth Century*. Ithaca, NY, Cornell University Press; reprinted New York, Russell and Russell, 1968.

Thill, A. 1987. *Jacob Balde. Odes (Lyrica)*, livres I–II. Mulhouse, Université de Haute-Alsace.

Thill, A. 1991. *Jacob Balde. Dix ans de recherché*. Paris, Champion.

Thill, A. 1993. 'Horace polonais, Horace allemand', in Ludwig 1993a: 381–425.

Thill, A. 1995. *Maciej Kazimierz Sarbiewski. Choix de poèmes lyriques*. Paris, Champion.

Thomas, R. F. 2011. *Horace. Odes IV and Carmen saeculare*. Cambridge, Cambridge University Press.

Tomlinson, C. 1993. 'Some Aspects of Horace in the Twentieth Century', in Martindale and Hopkins 1993: 240–57.

Traina, A. 1991. 'Orazio e Aristippo: le *Epistole* e l'arte di convivere', *RFIC* 119: 285–305; English version in Freudenburg 2009: 287–307.

Tränkle, H. 1993. 'Von Keller-Holder bis Shackleton Bailey: Prinzipien und Probleme der Horaz-Edition', in Ludwig 1993a: 1–29.

Turpin, W. 1998. 'The Epicurean Parasite: Horace, *Satires*, 1.1–3', *Ramus* 27: 127–40; reprinted in Freudenburg 2009: 122–37.

Vance, N. 1997. *The Victorians and Ancient Rome*. Oxford, Blackwell.

Vollmer, F. 1912. *Q. Horati Flacci. Opera*. Second edition, Leipzig, Teubner.

Wallace-Hadrill, A. 1985. *Suetonius*. London, Duckworth.

Wälli, S. 2002. *Melodien aus mittelalterlichen Horaz-Handschriften*. Kassel, Bärenreiter.

Watson, L. 1995. 'Horace's *Epodes*. The Impotence of *Iambos*?', in Harrison 1995a: 188–202.

Watson, L. 2003. *A Commentary on Horace's Epodes*. Oxford, Oxford University Press.

Wedde, I. 2003. *The Commonplace Odes*. Auckland, Auckland University Press.

West, D. 1967. *Reading Horace*. Edinburgh, Edinburgh University Press.

West, D. 1973. 'Horace's Poetic Technique in the *Odes*', in Costa 1973: 29–58.

West, D. 1995. *Horace Odes I. Carpe Diem*. Oxford, Oxford University Press.

West, D. 1997. *Horace. Odes and Epodes*. Oxford, Oxford University Press.

West, D. 1998. *Horace Odes II. Vatis Amici*. Oxford, Oxford University Press.

West, D. 2002. *Horace Odes III. Aere Perennius*. Oxford, Oxford University Press.

White, P. 1991. 'Maecenas' Retirement', *CPh* 86: 130–8.

White, P. 1993. *Promised Verse. Poets in the Society of Augustan Rome*. Cambridge, MA, Harvard University Press.

White, P. 2007. 'Friendship, Patronage and Horatian Sociopoetics', in Harrison 2007a: 195–207.

Wickham, E. C. 1874. *The Works of Horace. Volume 1*. Oxford, Clarendon Press.

Wickham, E. C. 1891. *The Works of Horace. Volume 2*. Oxford, Clarendon Press.

Wickham, E. C. 1900. *Horati Opera*. Oxford, Clarendon Press.

Wickham, E. C. and Garrod, H. W. 1912. *Horati Opera*. Oxford, Clarendon Press.

Williams, G. 1968. *Tradition and Originality in Roman Poetry*. Oxford, Oxford University Press.

Williams, G. 1969. *The Third Book of Horace's Odes*. Oxford, Oxford University Press.

Williams, G. 1972. *Horace*. Greece & Rome New Surveys in the Classics 6. Oxford, Oxford University Press.

Williams, G. 1974. Review of Brink 1971, *CR* 24: 52–7.

Williams, G. 1990. 'Did Maecenas "Fall from Favor"? Augustan Literary Patronage', in K. Raaflaub and M. Toher (eds.), *Between Republic and Empire. Interpretations of Augustus and His Principate*. Berkeley, CA/London, University of California Press: 258–75.

Williams, G. 1995. '*Libertino patre natus*: True or False?', in Harrison 1995a: 296–313; reprinted in Freudenburg 2009: 138–55.

Williamson, K. 1996. *The Poetical Works of Christopher Smart. Volume V. The Works of Horace, Translated into Verse*. Oxford, Oxford University Press.

Winter, U. 2002. *Jakob Balde. Liber Epodon*. Stuttgart, Teubner.

Wiseman, T. P. 1988. 'Satyrs in Rome? The Background to Horace's *Ars poetica*', *JRS* 79: 29–37.

Witke, C. 1983. *Horace's Roman Odes*. Leiden, Brill.

Woodman, A. J. 2002. '*Biformis Vates*: The *Odes*, Catullus and Greek Lyric', in Woodman and Feeney 2002: 53–64; reprinted in Woodman 2012: 41–58.

Woodman, A. J. 2009. 'Horace and Historians', *Cambridge Classics Journal (PCPhS)* 55: 161–71; reprinted in Woodman 2012: 112–20.

Woodman, A. J. 2012. *From Poetry to History. Selected Papers*. Oxford, Oxford University Press.

Woodman, A. J. and Feeney, D. (eds.) 2002. *Traditions and Contexts in the Poetry of Horace*. Cambridge, Cambridge University Press.

Woodman, A. J. and West, D. (eds.) 1984. *Poetry and Politics in the Age of Augustus*. Cambridge, Cambridge University Press.

Zetzel, J. E. G. 1980. 'Horace's *Liber Sermonum*: The Structure of Ambiguity', *Arethusa* 13: 59–77; reprinted in Freudenburg 2009: 17–41.

Ziolkowski, J. 2000. 'Nota Bene: Why the Classics Were Neumed in the Middle Ages', *Journal of Medieval Latin* 10: 74–102.

Ziolkowski, T. 2005. 'Uses and Abuses of Horace: His Reception since 1935 in Germany and Anglo-America', *IJCT* 12: 183–215.

INDEX